THE YORUBA SPIRITUAL TRAINING MANUAL

THE ULTIMATE RESOURCE GUIDE TO THE YORUBA RELIGION

AWO IFAGBEMI

First Edition: 2024.
Print. ISBN: 979-8-9909018-1-0
Library of Congress Control Number: 2024914247
Published by Michael Perez, Erie, PA, U.S.A.

To my wise elders in Ifa, from the bottom of my heart, thank you for all your support, wisdom, and guidance. Olodumare, the Orishas, my beloved mom, and my ancestors: In your light, I find guidance; in your wisdom, I find strength. You are my true guiding light in this world.

PREFACE
A SEEKER'S PATH: UNVEILING THE ORISHAS

My journey began as a quest for answers to life's questions, driven by an open mind and a deep desire to discover my purpose. This quest initially led me down various spiritual paths, each offering its own insight into the nature of existence. Over the years, I immersed myself in different philosophies and practices, hoping to find one that resonated with my inner being. I studied ancient knowledge, participated in various meditations, and sought guidance from several spiritual mentors. Each step taught me valuable lessons and provided insights into my own inner self. As my journey progressed, it became apparent that what I was searching for was not in any external teaching or doctrine but instead a way to heal my inner self and address my own trauma and pain. Over the past twenty years, I have realized that the true journey is one of introspection and self-discovery, peeling away layers of conditioning and societal expectations to uncover my authentic self, buried deep under years of social conditioning and trauma.

I discovered that alignment with my destiny is not a destination but a continuous process of inner growth and self-awareness. It requires listening to my inner voice, trusting my intuition, and embracing my unique path with courage and conviction. Many people, like me, find themselves searching for meaning, purpose, and healing in their lives. This quest is driven by the universal human need to understand our place in the world and live a life true to our essence. Ultimately, the journey of exploration is deeply personal. It teaches us that while external guidance can be helpful, the most profound answers come from within. This journey often leads us back to ourselves, revealing that we already possess the wisdom and strength needed to navigate our lives with purpose.

Throughout my exploration, I have come to believe that Orisha Spirituality, particularly Ifa divination, is one of the most effective ways we can unlock our inner potential and purpose. Rooted in ancient Yoruba tradition, this system emphasizes the interconnectedness of all life and the importance of maintaining balance and harmony within oneself, the universe, and within our human communities. Divination is not about predicting the future but instead about helping us to gain insight into our own current state of existence and understand how to re-align ourselves with our true potential.

By embracing Orisha Spirituality and engaging in Ifa divination, I have gained a deeper understanding of myself and my place in the world. This practice has helped me connect with my inner wisdom, cultivate my strengths, and overcome obstacles. It has become a cornerstone of my journey, guiding me toward a life of fulfillment and alignment with my true essence. Through this practice, I continue to grow, evolve, and navigate my journey with clarity and empowerment. This book on Yoruba spirituality serves as a comprehensive guide for readers seeking insight into this rich and ancient tradition. Join me on this journey as we explore further aspects of this beautiful tradition.

* * *

CONTENTS

The Sixteen Tenets of Orisha Spirituality   ix
Introduction   xi
Beliefs & Traditions   xvii

1. Exploring Yoruba Civilization   1
2. The Yoruba Concept of Divinity   11
3. The Orishas   17
4. The Concept of Atunwa   36
5. Honoring the Ancestors   42
6. At the Ancestors' Shrine   52
7. Spiritism: What Is It?   65
8. The Ori Consciousness   83
9. The Yoruba Calendar   97
10. Dreams and Spirit Guides   107
11. The Yoruba Life Cycle   113
12. Yoruba Initiation Rites and the Priestly Roles   120
13. Iwa-Pele and Omoluabi   130
    Communicating with the Spirits   135
14. Introduction to Divination   136
15. Understanding Ifá   142
16. The Yoruba Concept of Sacrifice   169
17. Ire and Ibi: Embracing Destiny's Balance   177
18. Introduction to Obi Divination   181
19. Obi Abata Divination   203
20. Osain and the Use of Plants   218
21. Finding a Spiritual Community   234

Glossary   237
Index   249
Bibliography   255
About the Author   259

THE SIXTEEN TENETS OF ORISHA SPIRITUALITY

These tenets form the foundation of our spiritual philosophy, guiding us in moral integrity. While they are widely shared across different lineages and groups, some tenets may be interpreted differently, and communities may practice them in ways that reflect their unique traditions and spiritual heritage.

THE SIXTEEN TENETS OF ORISHA SPIRITUALITY

1. *We believe in a supreme God called Olodumare or Olorun*
2. *We believe that Olodumare expresses divine will through universal laws and the divinities known as Orishas.*
3. *We believe all beings must follow the universal laws in nature established by Olodumare.*
4. *We believe we can communicate with Orishas and ancestors through divination, mediumship, and prophecy.*
5. *We believe that communication with the spiritual world through divination, mediumship, and prophecy is necessary for our well-being and survival here on earth.*

6. *We believe existence on earth operates according to natural laws of cause and effect and universal balance.*
7. *We believe in the concept of rebirth and the transmigration of the soul between the physical and spiritual realms.*
8. *We believe that we choose our own destiny before coming to earth.*
9. *We believe we can elevate our spiritual condition by aligning with our destiny, practicing good character, and communicating with the spiritual forces that support us.*
10. *We believe that our actions, virtues, and the destiny we choose most often determine our outcomes.*
11. *We respect the elders of our community for their wisdom on matters of life, survival, and spiritual counsel.*
12. *We believe that spiritual development is the goal of existence.*
13. *We view hope for the future as a virtue rather than fearing it.*
14. *We believe divination and sacrifice can provide insight and change the course of events.*
15. *The Golden Rule guides our lives; we strive to treat others as we wish to be treated.*
16. *The wisdom and knowledge we acquire propel us forward in life.*

* * *

INTRODUCTION
BEGINNING NOTES

In recent years, there has been an increase in interest in Orisha spirituality among those desiring to connect with the ancient ways of the past. The nature outside of us is, in fact, the same nature within. Many of us seek the wisdom of the ancients to rekindle our sacred connection to the divine Orishas, the sacred mother, and the energies of her life-giving womb, which we call planet earth. Connecting with the Orishas starts with honoring the earth and grounding ourselves so that we may heal. The sacred mother nature, her rhythms, and her seasons are not only the seasons of the year but also the seasons within us. We believe the forces of nature are attributes of divine beings.

Who are the Yoruba?

The Yoruba are in modern-day Nigeria. This is also the homeland of the spirits we call the Orishas. Over twelve million people were taken from this region into slavery, many being Yoruba men, women, and children. We have access to the Orishas here in the Western Hemisphere because the ancestors brought over a rich oral tradition that has had very few written sources up until recently. There is still much of this tradition that is not covered in books.

Among Yoruba spiritual practitioners, there is a strong belief not only in the Orishas but also in the spirits of deceased ancestors, known as Egun. These ancestors are believed to remain present in our lives, guiding us on Earth and helping us fulfill the destiny we chose before birth, which is understood to be the central purpose of life. However, during our time here, we often become distracted by less important concerns. In Yoruba thought, the ancestors, nature, and the Orishas are intimately involved in every human life, whether we consciously acknowledge their influence. The word Egungun refers to the collective ancestral spiritual force that supports and guides the living; the word Egun means "bone" in the Yoruba language, symbolizing lineage and continuity. Communication with Egun and the Orishas is carried out through various divination practices.

Orisha spirituality isn't merely a religion; it's a way of life that shapes our perspective on the world. It governs how we behave and how we perceive the things around us, including our respect for the Earth's ecosystem and respect for each other. It is common to see Orisha devotees getting involved in their communities to help make this world we all live in a better place. The Yoruba way of life influences how we engage with the world in every aspect. For instance, something as simple as cleaning up trash along the riverside holds spiritual significance. This act may be viewed as a form of sacrifice, symbolizing devotion or love for a specific Orisha. Additionally, it reflects our reverence and care for nature and the Earth we inhabit.

The Orishas are often seen by the Yoruba as aspects of the supreme God referred to as Olodumare, who tend to rule over various places or natural forces in nature, such as the river, woods, sky, etc. Let's take the example of the river used above. This is believed to be the domain of the Orisha Oshun. She is believed to not only rule over all the rivers on Earth but also all the fresh water on Earth. Oshun is seen as the divine force that rules over this natural element and is believed to manifest as it. Without fresh water, we would all die, and much of the life on earth would be unable to continue to survive. The power of Love is another significant aspect of Oshun's domain. Without love and passion, reproduction would be difficult. Love fosters emotional bonds between individuals, creating a sense of belonging and support which makes our existence more meaningful. It's believed that the Orishas contribute to making our world habitable, ensuring our comfort and well-being.

An Orisha devotee might offer a food item to Oshun by placing it near the riverside. They may do this by asking her to improve their love life. If someone desires a romantic partner or spouse, they may visit the river and leave an offering to seek Oshun's assistance in their pursuit. However, it is important to note that one should never leave plastic or other non-biodegradable items as offerings. Non-biodegradable items are not acceptable offerings and are seen as littering. This is considered disrespectful to both the Orishas and to the planet. Organic food items are seen as natural and permissible. Often, these items will become food for non-human critters. This is perhaps a way to give back to nature for all we take from her. Cleaning up the unnatural debris by the riverside, as mentioned in the example above, might also be perceived by an Orisha devotee as an attempt to earn Oshun's favor.

Last week, when I did my divination reading, it was told to me that I needed to leave some honey on the side of the river as a part of my offerings to Oshun. I asked if money could come my way during the reading. Honey and the honeybee are symbols of Oshun. Oshun helps with bringing not only love but sweetness into our lives, as well as wealth. Once I returned home, I noticed a honeybee inside my window trying to escape. I saw this as a sign that Oshun accepted the offerings that I left for her earlier that day. I happily caught the little honeybee and put it outside. For me, such an act became a form of devotion to this Orisha, demonstrating their eternal presence in our lives and their ongoing support.

These are some examples of how Orisha devotion operates under the Yoruba worldview. Such practices are a common part of everyday life for the Yoruba and for Yoruba practitioners living in the diaspora. As Orisha practitioners, we believe we have access to eternal guidance and wisdom. All we must do is tune into the natural cycle of the earth and the natural cycles of our own mind, body, and spirit. This wisdom and guidance is all around us. We just need to open ourselves up to receive it.

Have you ever realized that the ground you walk upon is sacred because the bones of the ancestors and those who have passed away before us are all buried beneath our feet?

We tend to say that it is the ancestors whose shoulders we stand upon; this can be taken literally when we stand upon the earth and walk upon the ground where their bones are, in fact, buried. It is true that almost all of humanity is buried in the ground beneath us, and yet we continue to live our daily lives walking from place to place without often realizing this fact. Nature can teach us truths about the world we otherwise would never have thought about prior. We just need to open our minds and disconnect from the human rat race construct of our complex modern society. No matter the challenges we face, it's likely someone in the past has walked a similar path, and this person is buried beneath our feet.

PART 2

CHAPTER SYNOPSIS: A GLIMPSE INTO THE JOURNEY AHEAD

Welcome to "The Yoruba Spiritual Training Manual." I invite you on a captivating exploration of the Yoruba people, their rich culture, and their fascinating belief system. We'll embark on a journey that unveils the mysteries of the Yoruba, delving into their history, mythology, and spiritual practices. In this book, we will go through the following:

Chapter 1, Exploring Yoruba Civilization, begins in the ancient city of Ile-Ife, considered the spiritual and cultural center of the Yoruba people. Here, we uncover the foundations of Yoruba culture, exploring their unique traditions and beliefs. Chapter 2, Unveils the Yoruba Concept of the Divine, delves into the multifaceted Yoruba concept of God. We explore their beliefs about the nature of the divine and the vital spiritual power known as "Ase" that underpins Yoruba spirituality.

Chapter 3, introduces over twenty powerful deities known as Orishas, who govern various aspects of life. Detailed descriptions and their unique associations bring these captivating entities to life. Chapters 4 through 6, teaches us how to connect with ancestors and explore the concept of "Atunwa," akin to reincarnation. We learn how the Yoruba honor their ancestors and foster a profound connection to their rich heritage.

In Chapter 7, we examine the philosophy of spiritism in Yoruba belief and its global impact. Discover how ordinary playing cards are used for divination, detailed at the end of the chapter. Chapters 8 and 9 explore "Ori," the Yoruba concept of spiritual consciousness, and the traditional Yoruba concept of Kojoda, revealing how time and destiny intertwine in Yoruba understanding.

Chapter 10 explores the realm of dreams and Egbe communities, while Chapters 11 through 13 delve into various life stages in traditional Yoruba society. From birth rituals to initiation ceremonies, we explore Yoruba definitions of morality and life passages.

Chapters 14 through 17 delve into intricate divination processes, exploring concepts like "Odu Ifa," sacrifice, "ire" (blessings), and "Osogbo" (misfortunes). We uncover how the Yoruba seek and maintain balance through these practices.

In Chapters 18 through 21, we will delve into the art of Obi divination and traditional Yoruba medicine. Finally, we will wrap up with what to look for in a spiritual community.

In conclusion, I hope that as you explore the Yoruba world further, you will develop a deep connection with the land, the ancestors, and the powerful mysteries embedded within the nature of the Orishas. Lastly, imagine yourself seeking refuge beneath the ancient boughs of a wise tree. Envision yourself connecting with this earth-based spirituality, forging a profound link with the land and the spirits of your ancestors who rest beneath your feet. Hush your racing thoughts and immerse yourself in communion with an ancient source of healing, a rhythmic pulse echoing the earth's very heartbeat. Embrace this journey and unlock the potent secrets held within the nature of the Orishas. Get ready to embrace yourself for an exciting adventure into this ancient faith of the Yoruba people.

BELIEFS & TRADITIONS

PART 1

CHAPTER I

EXPLORING YORUBA CIVILIZATION

IT'S WIDELY ACCEPTED that humanity originated in Africa. Nigeria is home to an ancient city called Ile Ife, believed to be the earliest known city. Some explorers have even likened it to the mythical lost city of Atlantis. This city holds immense significance in Yoruba culture, serving as the primal cradle of their civilization. In the mid-19th century, explorers were fascinated by artifacts discovered near Ile Ife, located in Osun State in the southwest part of Nigeria.

Speculating that these artifacts might be remnants of the mythical city of Atlantis, sparking scholarly discussion. The essence of Yoruba tradition lies in oral history, passed down through generations via spoken word until recent times when it was finally documented. For over a century, the Yoruba have preserved their cultural knowledge, myths, rituals, and beliefs through oral transmission before they were recorded in writing. Uncovering Yoruba History, we will start chapter one by delving into the history of the ancient Yoruba people from the Yoruba creation myth to all the way up to modern times. In the founding of the Yoruba civilization, let us first explore the Yoruba creation story, which has its foundation in oral tradition, as with many world traditions that are spread by word of mouth. The Yoruba creation myth has several different versions. The following version is the story that I am familiar with:

In the beginning, the universe was divided. Olorun, the all-powerful sky god, ruled the heavens above. Below, the vast and dark Earth, which was all ocean, belonged to Olokun. Olorun felt the need to create people and land on the earth below and decided to entrust Obatala with the task of shaping and creating land upon the watery Earth. At this time, the world was completely covered with water. Olorun gave Obatala permission to do this and did not inform Olokun. Olorun then gave Obatala several tools to complete his task, including a hen, a chameleon, and a snail shell with some dirt contained inside. Obatala then sought counsel from Orunmila, who provided him with many heavenly seeds from many different plants in heaven, including the seeds of the palm nut that Obatala would then plant upon the land once it was created.

Orunmila then gave Obatala a warning and told him to complete all he needed to do on the earth before returning to heaven. Obatala then went out to begin this task of creating land upon the earth, but he had to see Ogun first and give Ogun the silver Ogun needed to create a chain that Obatala could use to descend to the earth.Once Ogun forged the chain, Obatala began to climb down the chain from the heavens into the darkness below until the chain had no more length. The chameleon then instructed him to pour out the dirt he had contained in the snail shell to form dry land.

Obatala did this, and a mountain grew out of the ocean, forming dry land. Afterwards, he was instructed to let out the hen, which began spreading the dirt far and wide, making more dry land. He then released the chameleon from the bag to test the firmness of the ground and stepped onto the land to begin the task of planting the seeds. After a while, Obatala noticed the palm tree he planted earlier, from a palm nut, had become so tall that it reached the gates of heaven. He decided to climb the tree to rest in it for a little bit, so exhausted from his work.

After resting, he awoke to the sounds of the Orishas in heaven having a celebration and a feast. He also noticed all the beautiful fruit that grew upon the palm tree in its branches around him. Due to hunger and thirst, Obatala decided to attend the feast in heaven and forgot Orunmila's warning, but first gathered the palm fruit to bring to the party. Once Obatala arrived at the party, Shango and the other Orishas asked him what he had gathered, and Obatala told them that it was the fruit from the palm tree he planted upon the earth that grew so tall it reached the gates of heaven. Seeing how beautiful and delicious the fruit was after tasting it, the other Orishas decided to make an intoxicating and powerful alcoholic drink from the palm fruit Obatala had gathered, which they all drank.

Obatala became drunk and returned to earth to finish his work. When creating humans, due to drinking the palm wine, he became very careless and caused these people to be created deformed. Obatala then realized the error he had made and felt terrible remorse. He then called for Oduduwa, who descended to Earth. Obatala then put Oduduwa in charge of the earth. Oduduwa is believed to be the first king of the Yoruba people and the ancient city-state of Ile Ife. Many of the Orishas, as well as humans, continued to use the palm tree to travel back and forth from heaven to earth in those days. After creating people, Olokun became angry and did not want people upon the earth. Olokun made every attempt to eradicate the humans.

Olokun decided to challenge Obatala on who could make the most colorful tapestries. Obatala then sent down to Olokun's palace the chameleon, who, with his vibrant color-changing abilities, defeated Olokun in the challenge. From this day forward, Olokun allowed the earth to be used for human habitation.

* * *

The creation story teaches us how the Yoruba understand their origins and also offers important life lessons, particularly about responsibility and thoughtful decision-making. Obatala's journey illustrates the consequences of carelessness and reminds us to remain mindful of our actions and the choices we make. In the modern world, humanity has become increasingly careless in its treatment of the environment and the natural world on which we all depend, often driven by greed and the pursuit of power. Now more than ever, it is essential that we recognize this reality and change our ways before the damage becomes irreversible.

YORUBA HISTORY: FROM ILE IFE TO THE OYO EMPIRE

Tradition holds that Ile Ife was established around 1000 BCE, but evidence suggests people lived there even earlier. According to the Yoruba myth, Oduduwa, the first King of Ile Ife and of all Yoruba people, came from the heavens and governed humanity from the city, which was the world's first. Sixteen major Yoruba kingdoms, each led by descendants known as Obas (kings), emerged from Oduduwa's lineage. One of Oduduwa's descendants, Oranmiyan, played a crucial role in Yoruba history by expanding Yoruba influence. Around 500 BCE, Oranmiyan left Ile Ife and founded the powerful Oyo Empire to the north. Legend says a revered diviner guided him, and a sacred serpent led him to the site for Oyo. The Oyo Empire became a significant force in West Africa, known for its military strength, advanced administration, and economic prosperity. However, by the mid-18th century, Oyo's power had declined due to internal conflicts and the impact of the European Slave Trade, which saw millions of Africans enslaved and led to a decrease in its population.

Around 400 CE, Oyo rose to prominence in Yorubaland, with a notable migration from Ile Ife strengthening its military.

Between 500 CE and 1500 CE, the Yoruba civilization thrived, with Ile Ife and Oyo serving as important cultural and governance centers.

In the 15th and 16th centuries, the transatlantic slave trade began with the arrival of Europeans on the West African coast.

* * *

THE SLAVE TRADE

The Spread of Yoruba Culture to the Americas through the Trans-Atlantic Slave Trade occurred between the 15th and 17th centuries. During this period, more than four million people were sold into slavery and brought to the Caribbean and other parts of the Americas from Nigeria and other regions on the coast of West Africa. Many did not survive the journey across the ocean and perished deep in its waters. Many of the people who did survive fell terribly ill due to malnutrition and disease once they reached the shores of the Caribbean Islands. There is a belief today, as there was in the past, that the Orishas protected those ancestors who crossed the Atlantic. Unfortunately, many lost their lives on the journey across the ocean, but it is also believed that these ancestors are guarded by the Orishas who rule over the vast Ocean. Many believe that the Orishas still protect them today from the current oppression they face in modern times.

Arriving in the Americas, the Yoruba, like many other Africans, found themselves in a very strange land, with a culture, language, and strange belief system that they were totally unfamiliar with. They did not know where they were nor had any understanding of their

European captors. The Yoruba, like other West African Peoples brought to the Americas as slaves, struggled to keep the little identity they had from their homelands alive. The slave owners in the New World, on the other hand, did everything they could to rid the Africans of their own culture. They forced the slaves to become Christians and forbade them from speaking their native languages or practicing their native spirituality. The Slave traders went as far as to separate and mix people from different locations to prevent them from being able to recognize one another from the same place. This was intentionally done to prevent cultural or linguistic relations among the enslaved captives. What the Europeans failed to recognize is that there was a universal commonality among all Africans, regardless of what regional language they spoke or what area they came from. This commonality was found in the way they honored the spirits of nature.

<h2>RELIGIOUS AND CULTURAL SYNCRETISM</h2>

Syncretism emerged from the blending of traditions and beliefs among native Africans and the dominant cultures of Europeans and Native Americans in the New World. The Orisha spiritual tradition, encompassing various forms like Santeria, Candomblé, Ifa, Umbanda, Trinidad Orisha, or as it's known in Yoruba, Ìṣẹ̀ṣe ("tradition"), surprisingly, still thrives in rural Nigerian villages today, despite the presence of Christian and Muslim missionaries. This resilience underscores the enduring legacy of the Yoruba people. Similar traditions have spread to the Caribbean, North, South, and Central America due to the trans-Atlantic slave trade and the presence of Yoruba people in these regions.

These diaspora traditions are not purely Yoruba; they blend Yoruba spiritual practices with other cultural influences present in the regions where these traditions developed. These influences include Catholicism, Indigenous spiritual practices, Spiritism, and other beliefs and practices brought from various regions of Africa, such as

Congolese traditions from the Congo and Vodou from Dahomey. A notable illustration of this can be found in Cuba, where Catholic saints have been integrated with the Yoruba Orishas deities, as demonstrated in the following list of Orishas and their Catholic Saint Equivalencies:

- **Agayu** is synchronized with Saint Christopher.
- **Eleggua** is synchronized with Saint Anthony of Padua.
- **Ogun** is synchronized with Saint Peter.
- **Obatala** is synchronized with Our Lady of Mercy.
- **Shango** is synchronized with Saint Barbara.
- **Oshun** is synchronized with Our Lady of Charity.
- **Yemaya** is synchronized with Our Lady of Regla.
- **Orunmila** is synchronized with Saint Francis of Assisi.
- **Babalu Aye** is synchronized with Saint Lazarus.
- **Oya** is synchronized with Saint Theresa.
- **Osun** is synchronized with Our Lady of Charity.
- **Ochosi** is synchronized with Saint Norbert.
- **Osain** is synchronized with Saint Joseph.
- **Aggayu** is synchronized with Saint Christopher.
- **Nana Buruku** is synchronized with Saint Ann.
- **Yewa** is synchronized with Saint Claire of Assisi.
- **Erinle** is synchronized with Saint Sebastian.
- **Ibeji** is synchronized with Saints Cosmas and Damian.

It is crucial to acknowledge that the associations between Orishas and Catholic saints in Santeria/Lucumi practice in Cuba may differ among practitioners and regions. Another example of syncretism is the mixture of the Yoruba beliefs with the Native American beliefs. For instance, the use of tobacco smoke and corn as offerings to the Orishas and the honoring of the '*Ceiba Pentandra*' tree, traditionally revered by the Native Arawak tribes who resided in the

Caribbean. These elements merged into the modern-day tradition of Santeria.

- **Candomblé:** *Originating in Brazil, Candomblé centers on the worship of orixás, deities who represent various aspects of nature and human life. It incorporates elements of Yoruba, Fon, and other West African religions.*
- **Santería or Lukumi:** *Also known as Regla de Ocha, Santería is a syncretic religion that originated in Cuba. It centers on the worship of orishas, deities who represent various aspects of nature and human life and incorporates elements of Yoruba religion.*
- **Vodou:** *Also known as Voodoo, Vodou is a syncretic religion that originated in Haiti. It centers on the worship of loas, spirits who represent various aspects of nature and human life and incorporates elements of West African religions.*
- **Umbanda:** *Originating in Brazil, Umbanda combines elements of African, indigenous, and Christian beliefs. It centers on the worship of the orishás.*
- **Ifá:** *Ifá is a divination system and religious practice that originated from the Yoruba people of Nigeria and Benin. IFA is believed to be a divination Oracle made up of large sets of sacred verses and stories called Odus. Priests known as Babalawos interpret the messages using the sacred divination oracle that creates a specific pattern when thrown. The pattern that is created points to a specific Odu within the IFA tradition. Ifá is a part of the Yoruba religious tradition both in Africa and in the New World.*
- **Palo Mayombe:** *Palo Mayombe is an Afro-Cuban religion with origins in the Congo region of Central Africa. It focuses on the veneration of spirits known as Nkisi or Mpungo, which represent*

various aspects of nature and human life. Palo Mayombe
involves the use of natural objects which are seen as sacred. Palo
Mayombe practices include rituals, herbal medicine, and spirit
invocation.

- **Shango:** *A syncretic Yoruba-based tradition that originated in*
  Trinidad and Tobago, Shango centers on the worship of Shango,
  a Yoruba orisha associated with thunder and lightning. It
  incorporates elements of African, indigenous, and Christian
  beliefs.

* * *

FROM CONFLICT TO MODERNIZATION

Between the 1600s and the 1800s, the Yoruba were embroiled in persistent wars and conflicts with neighboring kingdoms and tribes, shaping the dynamics of the region. By the 1860s, British colonial forces had asserted complete control over what is now modern-day Nigeria, fundamentally altering the governance structure from traditional kingship to a colonial administration. This colonial rule persisted for a century until Nigeria finally gained independence in 1960. However, the aftermath of colonialism presented the Yoruba people with new challenges. From the 1990s onward, they grappled with the dual task of preserving their rich cultural heritage while simultaneously adapting to the demands of a rapidly modernizing and globalized society. This period marked a significant juncture in Yoruba history, characterized by a continuous struggle for identity in the face of profound socio-political changes.

In conclusion, gaining a brief understanding of Yoruba history is not only valuable for comprehending Orisha spirituality but also for grasping the diverse influences that have shaped its evolution. Yoruba spirituality is deeply embedded within the cultural, social, and historical fabric of the Yoruba people. By delving into historical events, cultural practices, and societal structures, we can unravel the significance and meaning behind various spiritual concepts, rituals, and deities. For instance, knowledge of Yoruba history illuminates the origins of key spiritual traditions, such as the worship of Orishas, and sheds light on their roles within Yoruba society.

Moreover, historical events, uch as the establishment of the Oyo Empire or the impact of colonialism, may have influenced the trajectory of Yoruba spiritual practices over time. Understanding Yoruba history also offers insights into the resilience and adaptability of Yoruba spirituality in the face of external pressures. It allows us to appreciate the complexities and nuances of Yoruba spiritual traditions, recognizing them as dynamic systems that have evolved in response to changing historical and social contexts. In essence, a brief understanding of Yoruba history serves as a pathway to spiritual enlightenment, enabling us to appreciate the intricate connections between the Yoruba people, their history, and their spiritual beliefs.

* * *

CHAPTER 2

THE YORUBA CONCEPT OF DIVINITY

IN THIS CHAPTER, we will further discuss some basic concepts found in Yoruba Cosmology. According to the Yoruba, we come to earth to fulfill a destiny we chose for ourselves in heaven. During our time here, we face continual tests that help us spiritually develop and accumulate "*Ase*" or "*Ashe*" (pronounced Ah-Shay), which means power or command. The Yoruba also believe that each person has a unique purpose, chosen in the heavens before birth. Earthly life is an opportunity to grow spiritually and become the best version of ourselves. Through life's challenges, we gain Ase, a spiritual force that empowers us to command our own destinies.

The Yoruba describe *Ase* as the magical power God gave to the Orishas to help create the universe. God is considered pure *Ase*. This power can be collected and accumulated, and Orisha devotees believe it can be acquired by consulting the Orishas through divination, following one's chosen destiny, practicing good character (Iwa Pele), avoiding taboos, and performing necessary sacrifices (ebbos) to realign one's life if off course. These practices help accumulate more *Ase*. This power, given to the Orishas by God, is then bestowed upon humans and animals for righteous actions.

Maintaining and accumulating *Ase* is crucial for spiritual well-being. Improper behavior can lead to a loss of this power, resulting in illness or loss of blessings. *Ase* permeates all aspects of creation and functions as a spiritual currency in both 'Aye' (earth) and 'Orun' (heaven). The word Ase is often used at the end of prayers or rituals to seal their power, like saying "amen" in Abrahamic traditions. Through divination and ebbo, the Orishas provide guidance and courage to overcome life's difficulties, ensuring the natural balance and fair distribution of *Ase*. The Yoruba believe in personal responsibility for one's actions. The Orishas, created by Olodumare, help govern and maintain the universe, guiding individuals to live correctly and accumulate Ase for spiritual growth and balance.

THE YORUBA CONCEPT OF GOD

The Yoruba people refer to God by three different names: Olodumare, Olorun, and Olofin. These names represent various aspects of God's nature and manifestations.

OLODUMARE

Olodumare is often seen as the supreme God, the creative force of the universe, and the possessor of all Ashe (spiritual power). Olodumare decides how Ashe is distributed and is viewed as distant from humanity, neither male nor female, and the ultimate owner of the universe. As the eternal author of time, Olodumare is the creator of virtue, morality, and natural law, which the Orishas enforce to maintain balance. By respecting Olodumare's laws and practicing Iwa pele (good character), humans honor God, bringing balance and blessings into their lives through the granting of Ashe. Practicing Iwa pele is the most direct form of worship to Olodumare. While Olodumare grants humans free will, the Orishas, who maintain natural balance, do not have total free will and can punish humans for violating divine laws. Olodumare governs the destiny of all beings, acting as the master architect of the universe.

OLORUN

Olorun is the aspect of Olodumare that rules heaven and the afterlife. Humans experience this aspect only after death and do not worship Olorun directly. The name "Olorun" means the ruler of Orun (heaven) and is often associated with the sun, particularly in Yoruba traditions like Santeria and Candomblé. Olorun created the world and the Irunmole, governing destiny, and is known as "Oba-Orun" (king of the sky).

OLOFIN

Olofin represents the aspect of God that governs creation and the Ashe within it. This aspect allows events to occur and manifest in the universe. Olofin grants permission for all happenings and rules over the Ìmólè (Forces of Nature) and all beings in the physical world.

OUR RELATIONSHIP WITH THE ORISHAS

The Orishas could be looked at as both aspects of Olodumare and intermediaries between us and Olodumare. This relationship is also not considered one-sided but instead one with a mutual covenant where man agrees to provide offerings and honor in return for help. It is said that there are 400 plus one Orishas on one side of Olodumare, and on the other side, 400 plus one Ajogun or demonic forces meant to trick living beings. The plus one after 400 symbolizes that there is a continuation of new Orishas coming into existence based on a new being elevated to Orisha status or one being created. The same is true for demonic entities. However, demonic entities have accrued so many bad deeds that they tend to be reborn into a state of a destructive nature spirit. These nature spirits are controlled by the

13

Orishas. The word Orisha comes from two words: Ori, meaning head, and 'sa', meaning senior or guardian. The term Orisha can be understood as a senior or wise head.

The term "Irunmole" translates to what we would call the "primordial beings." Irunmole are considered primordial beings created by Olodumare before the world existed. They are believed to have assisted Olodumare in the creation of the universe and are regarded as ancient and powerful divine entities. The Irunmole encompass a broader category of primordial beings or divine spirits in Yoruba cosmology. They are the original Orishas that have existed since the creation of the world and assisted Olodumare in its formation.

Non-Irunmole Orishas are often associated with specific historical or mythical narratives and are believed to have originated from various sources, including ancestral spirits, cultural heroes, and natural phenomena. Some notable Irunmoles include: *Obatala, Orunmila, Ogun, Yemoja, Oshun, Sango, and Esu:*

- **Obatala**: He is revered as the father of all Orishas and embodies purity, wisdom, and creation. He is often depicted in white clothing, wielding a staff and palm frond.
- **Orunmila**: Serves as the Orisha of wisdom, divination, and destiny, guiding believers through the Ifa oracle with his divination chain and tray.
- **Ogun**: Known as the Orisha of iron, warfare, and technology, is depicted as a powerful warrior wielding a machete or sword, representing tools, industry, and metalworking.
- **Yemoja**: The Orisha of the ocean, motherhood, and fertility, is revered as the protector of women and children, symbolized by shells, fish, and the crescent moon.

- **Oshun:** Associated with love, beauty, and prosperity, is depicted adorned in gold and symbolizes fertility, sensuality, and abundance through mirrors, fans, and honey.
- **Sango:** Representing thunder, lightning, and fire, embodies courage, strength, and justice, often depicted with a double-headed axe amidst flames.
- **Esu:** Also known as Elegua, serves as the Orisha of crossroads, communication, and trickery, facilitating communication between the human and divine realms as the guardian of pathways.

* * *

The Irunmole are highly respected within Yoruba spirituality and are honored for their power and ability to influence the natural world. They are often invoked in prayers and rituals, sought after for guidance. Beyond shaping the world, they are credited with imparting essential knowledge, such as agriculture, medicine, and the arts, to humanity on earth.

WHAT IS THE SACRED DUALITY?

Once upon a time, it was believed that heaven and earth existed as one interconnected realm, visible and accessible to humans. People could freely traverse between the heavenly and earthly domains, passing through a veil. However, as time passed, greed tainted the hearts of humanity. They approached the heavenly realm with impurity and disrespect, angering Olorun, the divine ruler. After enduring this disrespect for a period, Olorun commanded Eshu, the Orisha of the crossroads, to create a division between the two worlds using a dark abyss. From then on, humans could only traverse between realms through rebirth.

. . .

The concept of Sacred Duality in Yoruba spirituality acknowledges the interconnectedness of the physical and spiritual realms, a reflection of the duality within us. It emphasizes that actions in one realm can affect the other, emphasizing the importance of balance and harmony. This interconnectedness is demonstrated through rituals such as offering food to ancestors, believing that they, in turn, support and guide us. Communication with Orishas, ancestors, and spirits through divination, prayer, and sacrifice is believed to bring Ase, or spiritual power. Maintaining balance is crucial for the proper functioning of both realms; disruptions can lead to illness or misfortune. Thus, Yoruba religion stresses the necessity of balance and harmony to ensure well-being in both the physical and spiritual worlds.

CHAPTER 3
THE ORISHAS

IN THE YORUBA RELIGION, there are powerful deities known as Orishas. The term "Orisha" is composed of two parts: "Ori," meaning head, and "-sha," meaning guardian. Together, they roughly translate to "guardians of the head." As we explored in previous chapters, Orishas serve as intermediaries between humanity and the supreme god, Olodumare. Traditionally, Olodumare is perceived as distant from humans and the world, leading to the belief that Orishas were created to oversee the world on Olodumare's behalf. However, some Yoruba spiritual traditions offer a different perspective, seeing Olodumare as the all-encompassing consciousness of creation, which includes the Orishas themselves, rather than a distinct entity.

THE DAY THE POWERS FELL FROM THE SKY

As the universe expanded, the Orishas sought control over it. To settle their rivalry, Olodumare made a decree:

The powers shall fall like scattered seed.
Whoever catches them first shall reign,

The strongest shall rise, the rest shall remain.
Orunmila announced the fateful day,
The Orishas gathered, eager to play.

From the heavens, the gifts rained down,
And the Orishas scrambled across the ground.
Some were swift, some fell behind,
Yet each received what fate assigned.
Thus, their powers were set in place,
Each Orisha, with divine embrace.

* * *

In connection to the story, it is agreed upon by all Orisha practitioners that the Orishas have the responsibility and power to oversee Olodumare's creation. They exist to ensure that the laws of nature and of balance are upheld and kept in place. The Yoruba believe everything in the universe is governed by cause-and-effect relationships, including our actions, and that every interaction we engage in is an energy exchange that changes the universal balance at every moment.

The Orishas possess the power to guide, protect, bless, and even punish, if need be, and work to constantly restore this balance. Their powers to punish or bless tend to stay within the confines of our actions here on earth, as well as our alignment towards our destiny. Essentially, what we put out into the universe by way of our actions, we get back. This concept is like the law of Karma believed by many Eastern Philosophies. Each Orisha is also understood to have its own distinct association with various natural phenomena, its unique personality, sacred objects, symbols, colors, and foods, as well as various taboos. These traits are often reflected in nature, which is associated with various Orishas.

By honoring and celebrating the Orishas, we can connect with Olodumare and the forces of nature, gaining insight into how to live a fulfilling life. The Orishas represent a source of pride and a connection to African heritage, and their worship and celebration serve as a means of cultural resistance and preservation. The Orishas are accessible to all, regardless of social status, and guide us on a spiritual journey towards fulfilling our destiny.

DESCRIPTIONS OF THE MOST COMMON ORISHAS IN THE YORUBA BELIEF SYSTEM

Below is a list of the Orishas that are most frequently honored within Yoruba culture, as well as the diaspora spiritual traditions. Each Orisha is accompanied by a description to help provide a better understanding of their significance.

AGANJU

Aganju is a deity closely connected to the Orisha Shango, and in Yoruba land, he is often seen as one of the historical kings of the Oyo Empire. He is also associated with Saint Christopher, whose feast day is on the 25th of July. His name comes from the Yoruba word "Aganju," which means wilderness, and he is seen as the ruler over terrains where very little life can survive, such as volcanoes, deserts, caves, and mountain peaks.

Aganju is also associated with fire and lava and helps those who honor him overcome their difficulties in life. He gives his devotees the strength to persevere through challenging times and helps them come out victorious. Aganju is believed to have helped enslaved Africans survive slavery and defeat their oppressors, and he also helps travelers get to their destinations safely. He is commonly called upon in times where strength, stability, and grounding are needed, as well as times where transformation and change are necessary for survival. Aganju is believed to be the force of transformation and change.

AJE

The Orisha of wealth and prosperity. She is associated with abundance, good fortune, and the power of manifestation. Her attributes include financial prosperity, the Cowrie shell, commerce, and material abundance. She is also associated with the earth and fertility, as well as with feminine energy and intuition. In some traditions, Aje is believed to be a wise and powerful healer, and her energy is often invoked for blessings related to money, business success, and general good fortune. Offerings include Pigeons, Flowers, a Glass of water, Jewelry, Cowrie shells, Money, incense, and candles.

AYANGALU

It is believed that this Orisha was the first drummer and played what is known as the talking drum. The talking drum is commonly played in Yoruba ceremonies and at celebrations. It is a crucial part of Yoruba culture and spiritual life. It is believed that Ayangalu speaks through the drums by possessing the drummers. The patterns the drumming makes can be interpreted by his initiates.

BABALU-AYE

Babalú-Aye is the spirit of the Earth and is associated with both infectious disease and healing. Babalú-Aye rules over illness and can both cure and cause disease. He is connected to iku/death. He is seen as the force of nature responsible for bringing and curing diseases. He is commonly offered grain. He is associated with brown stones, such as jasper and tiger's eye, and natural brown clay used to make pottery. Offerings include palm oil, goats, pigeons, and roosters.

DADA

Dada is the elder sister of Shango, while others consider her to be connected to Obatala. Dada is often revered as the Orisha of mother-hood, fertility, and the well-being of unborn children. She is believed to play a crucial role in the development and nurturing of the human embryo. This Orisha is one of the lesser-known Orishas but is strongly associated with fertility and childbirth and is widely recog-nized as a symbol of motherhood and the loving care of children. Additionally, some view Dada as the embodiment of the power of fertility and the cycle of life, including the continual process of birth and rebirth after death.

ERINLE

Erinle, also known as Inle, is an Orisha associated with health, medicine, hunting, and the estuary where the sea meets fresh water. Erinle/Inle is often considered the patron of gay and transgender people and is syncretized with the Archangel Raphael in the dias-pora. He is depicted as a strong, androgynous warrior and hunter adorned in cowrie shells, coral, and feathers, with snakes around him. He is the deity of health and medicine, the physician to all other deities, and the hunter of the land and sea. As a skilled healer and physician who employs herbal medicine, he is seen as an Orisha that protects the deaf and Lesbian, Gay, Bisexual, and transgender people.

He is often called upon for protection and healing by doctors and other types of healers within the Orisha tradition. His shrine often consists of stones sourced from the Erinle River. Offerings include shells, fish, pigeons, guinea fowl, various flowers and herbs, a glass of water, and candles.

ESU/ELEGUA

In Yoruba Orisha spirituality, Esu is a highly important Orisha. He is believed to be the messenger between God and all other Orishas and is also known as the owner of all roads and paths. In ceremonies and rituals, it is important to first honor Esu before moving forward, as he is the one who delivers sacrifices to God and other Orishas. Esu is also considered a divine balancer and trickster who could open doors for communication with the spirit world.

He is often depicted holding a set of keys, which were given to him by God, and is said to have the power to view the past, present, and future. Offerings include male goats, cornmeal, cigars, toasted corn, coconuts, roosters, palm oil, kola nuts, pigeons, strong alcohol, a cup of coffee, candles, a glass of water, incense, and tobacco, to name a few. Elegua is sometimes seen as a different Orisha, but is a path of Esu known as Esu-elegbara. Esu is often seen as a trickster who takes many different forms and appearances. Sometimes he takes the form of a child, while other times he may appear as an old man. Esu often plays many different roles and often manifests based on which role he is playing within the cosmos. Esu can open and close doors; he is the one who holds the keys to every door. He is also able to facilitate communication with the spirit world and deliver offerings to the other divinities. Natural stones associated with this Orisha are Jasper, black onyx, red garnet, and Yangi Stone. Taboos of Eshu include whistling around him and using profanity around him.

IBEJI

The Ibeji or Jimaguas is the Orisha of the divine twins. Twins are seen as sacred to the Yoruba. It is said that twins are connected, and if one passes away before the other, this could affect the living twin. It is believed that twins have a very special spiritual connection. A statue is carved out of wood after the death of one of the twins so that the mother and the other twin can honor the spirit of the deceased twin.

The twins represent duality and balance between both male and female, as well as within nature. The first-born twin is often named Taiwo, which means "taste of life," and the second-born twin, Kehinde, which means "who comes last." Ibeji statues often come in pairs, one male and one female. Pataki tells us the origins of the Ibeji when Oshun gave birth to them and feared being ridiculed because twins were uncommon. She denied being their mother. The Ibeji were taken in by Oya and later went to live with Yemaya. It is said that whoever receives the Ibeji will be blessed by them. It is common in the diaspora to give this Orisha upon initiation or for protection. Offerings include a glass of water, fruit, candies, cake and sweets, toys, and candles, among others. One taboo with the Ibeji is that one should always feed them both together.

IROKO

A spirit that inhabits the Iroko tree, Milicia Excelsa in Africa, and the ceiba tree, or the silk cotton tree, in the diaspora. It is believed that spirits can take rest under the branches of the ceiba tree by the Native Indigenous peoples of the Caribbean. When the Africans arrived, they saw the Ceiba tree as another variation of the Iroko tree, which only existed in Africa. It is believed that if the Ceiba or the African Milicia Excelsa are cut down, it can bring great misfortune to the entire community.

NANA BULUKU

She is commonly worshiped in Benin and Dahomey by the Fon people. She is considered the supreme goddess who gave birth to Mawu and Lisa in many Vodou lineages. In the Yoruba diaspora, she is often honored as a female aspect of Olodumare. Her symbols are the moon and the earth. She is seen as the wise grandmother to all of life as well as to all the Orishas, linked to the aspects of the divine feminine: the maiden or youth, the mother or middle age, and the grandmother or elder. All living things begin life at birth, then transition into youth, motherhood, elderhood, and finally pass away. It is said that this cycle of growth and transformation is what Nana rules over. She is also associated with fertility, stability, and abundance from the earth.

OBA

She was considered the oldest of the Orisha Shango's wives. The story says she was tricked into cutting off her ear and feeding it to Shango to put him under a love spell due to rivalry with Shango's other wives, Oya and Oshun. It was Oshun who was Shango's favorite wife; however, Oshun was filled with jealousy over Oba due to her being the eldest of all the wives. It was said her descendants would inherit the crown. She told Oba that she, in fact, cut off a piece of her ear and fed it to him many years prior, and this is why she became his favorite. Following Oshun's advice, Oba decided to do this and cut off her entire ear. When Shango found out, he was furious at Oba and dismissed her as one of his wives. Out of grief, it is said she turned into what is today the Oba River, located in Nigeria. She rules over marriage and relationships. Offerings include pigeons, female goats, and a glass of water.

OBATALA

Obatala is often depicted as the father of all the Orishas and is associated with the color white, representing purity. Obatala is regarded as the creative force in the universe. It is said that he descended from the heavens on a chain, carrying with him all the items needed for creating the world and humanity. He is often depicted as a wise old man dressed in a white robe, possessing a staff and a crown. Obatala is believed to be the one who molds the child in the womb. In the beginning, it is told that he was put in charge of creating human beings, but while molding them, he became drunk on the palm wine, resulting in humans becoming deformed when he created them. Even though this was the case, it is still believed that Obatala is the source of all that is just, peaceful, wise, compassionate, and harmonious in the universe, and rules over cleanliness. Often, only white and pure things are given to him as offerings.

His sacred places within nature are hills, places with high elevation, and mountains. These locations are often where offerings are left for him. Often known as the Orisha of the white cloth, his preferred color is white. He helps to enforce justice in the world. Obatala is considered gender-fluid, with some of his paths being male while others are female. He also rules over all human heads and determines what is considered good and not good character in the world. One of his symbols is the snail, and as the snail is one of the slowest creatures to move, Obatala teaches his followers the importance of patience in life and the importance of self-discipline. His children do not use alcohol or mind-altering drugs; these things are taboo to them. Various stones associated with him are Moonstone, White quartz, Clear quartz, Silver, lead, and opal. Offerings include white goats, doves, white pigeons, cotton, coconut, cascarilla, cocoa butter, rice, white foods, flowers, candles, white cloth, snails, silver coins, silver jewelry, and pears. Taboos of Obatala include salt, palm wine, and black balm kernel oil.

ODUDUWA

The Yoruba people consider Oduduwa to be both a historical figure and an Orisha. He served as the first King or Ooni of the Yoruba empire, ruling over the city-state of Ife, which is where the Yoruba empire originated. It is also believed to be the first city on earth. Many Yoruba people believe that Oduduwa taught them the Orisha religion and played a crucial role in the creation of the world and human beings. As a result, he is regarded as the father of the entire Yoruba people and civilization, and he is revered as a wise and powerful king and Orisha. According to Yoruba mythology, Oduduwa descended from the sky on a chain to the earth at the time of its creation. He is often seen as the Orisha who established the leadership of Kings and societal order upon the earth by those who honor him.

OGUN

Ogun is one of the most popular Orishas in the Yoruba religion. He is venerated in Yoruba tradition and in other traditions, such as within Vodun as Ogou. He is known for ruling over war, iron, hunting, and agriculture, and is often prayed for by his followers for protection when heading into the battlefield. Ogun is seen as a warrior, a wood carver, and a blacksmith, and rules over these professions.

He is often depicted with a large machete in his hand and is associated with strength and endurance, as well as the transformation that one would go through as a warrior or in life when overcoming obstacles or challenges and coming out victorious. Iron is considered one of his most sacred symbols. He is also associated with dogs. Sometimes his devotees will leave offerings for him at the railroad tracks. Offerings include the same as Eshu: male goats, roosters, pigeons, palm oil, yams, rum, plantains, guinea pepper, red pepper, water, alcohol, iron, metal trinkets, and metal jewelry, candles to name a few. Ogun is seen as ruling over the domain of technology and is thought to have taught humanity how to use it. It is also believed that during the creation of the world, Ogun cleared the path with his machete on the way down to the earth so that the other Orishas were able to enter the world. His colors are often black and green. Natural stones associated with this Orisha are iron, meteorites, hematite, magnetite, and pyrite due to the high concentrations of iron in all these stones. One taboo with Ogun is offering him Adin Dudu or Black Palm Kernel oil.

OKE

He is often associated with the Orisha Obatala, where it is said these two Orishas are inseparable. He is associated with extremely high mountains, peaks, and places in the natural world. He is believed to have a fair complexion and is known to keep watch over the world and the other Orishas. He is prayed to by travelers for protection on their journey. He is sometimes present with Obatala during crowning and initiation ceremonies. The word Òké translates to mean top or highest point. It is said he speaks through Obatala in divination.

OKO

Oko is associated with agriculture and farming. He is called upon by farmers and agriculturalists. He is also associated with the land and is considered the patron Orisha of farmers. He is called upon to help farmers have a bountiful harvest. He is often called upon also to bring prosperity and abundance to those who work with the land. He teaches us how to cultivate the fields of our lives. Offerings include roosters, pigeons, fruits, and vegetables harvested by farmers.

OLOKUN

Olokun lives in the deep and dark parts of the ocean near the bottom, where her palace is located. During the creation story, Olokun was upset about the idea of having humans on the earth. After a competition she waged with Olorun, she agreed to permit humans to inhabit the earth. Olokun is associated with immense wealth and prosperity and embodies the darkest part of the ocean. Her beauty is admired by all, and she works closely with Yemaya, believed by some to be her sibling. Olokun is sometimes believed to be chained to the bottom of the ocean to prevent her anger from shaking the earth. Colorful textiles and beautiful art are often associated with her and the deep, vivid colors of the ocean. Olokun is sometimes seen as the owner of hidden treasures and secret magical knowledge. Offerings include pigeons, roosters, shells, and colorful beads.

OLORI-MERIN

Olori-merin is considered the Orisha who rules over the four cardinal points of the universe. He oversees, looks over, and watches the universe and all things that exist. He also rules over the many-dimensional planes that make up the universe. He has been called in other traditions the one who rules over the "four quarters or the four watchtowers".

ORUNMILA

Orunmila is a very important Orisha in the Yoruba faith, especially to Babalawos and Iyanifas, who are the priests and priestesses of Orunmila. Orunmila is viewed as the Orisha of Wisdom, Knowledge, and, of course, IFA Divination. Orunmila was the first Babalawo when he walked upon the earth and took the form of a human being. Orunmila is called upon by IFA Priests for his wisdom during the IFA Divination process.

The Babalawos (male) and Iyanifas (female) are his priests, and they are initiated in his name. Note: There are many priests in the Orisha tradition who are initiated into many different Orishas. These priests are commonly referred to as Olorishas or Babalorishas (male) and Iyalorishas (female), but they are not Babalawos or Iyanifas unless they become initiated or are "crowned" to Orunmila. Then they can be called Babalawo or Iyanifa. The Babalawos or Iyanifas could be crowned into the mysteries of another Orisha and become a priest of that Orisha, called an Olorisha priest, before initiating to Orunmila and becoming a Babalawo or Iyanifa.

However, once they initiate into Orunmila, they often serve solely as IFA priests or as Babalawos at that point. Orunmila is often associated with insight, knowledge, wisdom, and the ability to see into the future. Many people go to his priests for guidance. It is believed that all the other Orishas seek out help from Orunmila and guidance from IFA when in need. Orunmila is said to be a witness to all destinies and took part in helping Olodumare (God) in creating the universe. Some say Orunmila is Olodumare's wisdom. Individuals initiated to him often wear beads colored green and yellow or green and brown, depending on which Yoruba tradition. Natural stones associated with Orunmila include emerald, Tiger's eye, Jade, Peridot, and green tourmaline. Offerings also include goats, pigeons, palm oil, Shea butter, gin, fruits, honey, water guinea fowl, coconuts, Kola nuts, Incense, a glass of water, candles, and cornmeal. One taboo with Orunmila is offering him Adin Dudu or Black Palm Kernel oil.

OSAIN

Osain, sometimes referred to as Osanyin, is the Orisha of herbs, healing plants, and all things related to herbal medicine. He is often called upon for help by Orisha priests and those needing help with healing or suffering from an illness. These people will often go to their priests for help after seeing a diviner and a doctor. Osain often appears as a spirit or a human man covered in vines and leaves, and he possesses a staff that he carries with him. It is believed that Osain knows the healing properties of all the plants, mushrooms, and other natural substances ever created. He has the power to determine if a plant or other natural substance can heal an illness or not. He can also change the properties of plants to make them ineffective for healing or transform them into powerful medicines. His domain is the forest, and those who honor him are often in the healing professions, including doctors, botanists, pharmacists, herbalists, healers, magicians, diviners, and chemists. Some offerings to Osain include various flowers and leaves of plants, tobacco, and alcohol. Osain's staff, commonly called his opere, is often used for blessing, healing, and cleansing.

OSHOSI

Oshosi is considered the Orisha of hunting, justice, and truth. He also lives in the forest and is the patron Orisha of hunters. He is commonly called upon to help deliver truth and justice in various legal and moral matters. Many turn to Oshosi in pursuit of truth, justice, and protection, especially if an injustice has occurred. Oshosi is said to be fair and direct. It is believed that Oshosi's bow and arrow never miss their target. Legend has it that Oshosi was once human and was elevated to the status of an Orisha due to his sense of justice. Oshosi often goes hunting with Ogun. His colors are green and blue. Offerings to Oshosi often include goat, pig, and guinea fowl, pigeons, as well as various fruits such as plantains, pears, mangoes, gin, or other alcoholic spirits, avocados, papayas, a glass of water, and candles. Oshosi is often given the same offerings as Ogun.

One taboo with Oshosi is offering him Adin Dudu or Black Palm Kernel oil.

OSHUN

Oshun, one of the most beloved Orishas in Yoruba land, is often associated with rivers, streams, and flowing fresh water in Nigeria, as well as in the diaspora. She is the Orisha of love, beauty, sensuality, and attraction, and many people ask for her help with these things. Oshun is known as the bringer of the sweet things in life, including opulence, wealth, beauty, love, longevity, attraction, festivities, and luxury. She is also seen as a powerful healer, especially when it comes to emotional healing, and a protector of women and children. Oshun is said to own all the fresh water on Earth, and people often honor her at the river, where they leave her various gifts of food and other items in return for her help. Oshun also rules over the circulatory system of the body. Some offerings given to Oshun include melons, oranges, pigeons, sugar, honey, bananas, brown sugar, grapefruit, mirrors, sunflowers, and any yellow flowers, a glass of water, candles, and incense. Some natural stones associated with Oshun are amber, citrine, gold, and topaz.

OSUMARE

Osumare is often viewed as the Orisha who transforms into rainbows and serpents; he rules over both. It is believed that his presence marks renewal, hope, new beginnings, release from negative energy or curses, purification, and fresh starts. His presence is also believed to bring serenity and calmness after the storm, which may be the turbulence and storms in our own lives. According to Yoruba tradition, Olodumare told Osumare to create a sign in the sky that all can see to signify that the creation of both heaven and earth had been completed. Osumare then created the first rainbow in the sky for all to see. Some of the various elements that Osumare rules over include naturally occurring cycles such as sunshine, cloudiness, evaporation, condensation, and precipitation of water. The serpent is sometimes presented in ceremonies as a representation of Osumare's presence because of its powerful ability to remove curses or negative energies from the person who comes in close contact with the serpent. Osumare is also said to spend half of his time as a male while the other half as a female. Because of this, Osumare is often seen as androgynous. He is said to watch over and protect children, creative people, such as artists, and those who are transgender are all under the protection of Osumare. Also, the umbilical cord is often seen as a symbol of Osumare. When a child is born, the umbilical cord is often buried, not destroyed, or thrown away as a symbol of respect. Offerings to Osumare include fresh water, flowers, honey, various fruits such as watermelon, incense, mangoes, papaya, yellow candles, small carvings of serpents, white or painted colored eggs, and duck. Offerings are often placed near large waterfalls where rainbows can be seen. Stones associated with this Orisha include Quartz Crystal, Opal, Moonstone, Labradorite, and Sun Stone.

OYA

The Orisha Oya or Yansa rules over the wind, which she can transform into tornadoes and hurricanes. Oya also rules over the marketplace and is the protector and guardian of the dead. She is the mother of Egungun and helps the ancestors transition to the afterlife. The powers of Oya often bless people with heightened intuition. For her children and those who respect the ancestors, she often blesses them with the powers of clairvoyance and the ability to communicate with the dead, as well as a heightened sense of intuition. Oya's energy is present at the gates of the cemetery, symbolizing the barrier between life and death. This is the location where offerings are often left for her. Oya rules the force of nature that brings sudden and abrupt changes in people's lives, especially if something needs to change in that person's life. She gives a lot of warning beforehand. It is important we trust our intuition. This change can often be felt as distressing and chaotic, but following it comes new beginnings, renewal, and growth. Sometimes Oya will present in people's lives like a whirlwind because the person has not addressed an aspect of their life in need of change. Other times, Oya will present herself in someone's life as a fierce protector, defending the person from harm. She is a warrior and has a strong motherly love for those she cares for. Oya is seen as one of the powerful witches as well. Offerings to her include plums, eggplants, grapes, raisins, copper coins, female goats, and jewelry. Amethyst and copper are stones associated with her. A taboo of Oya is offering her ram.

SHANGO

The Orisha Shango, also known as Sango or Chango, is a highly revered deity in Yoruba spirituality. Some believe he has two forms: as a historical King of Oyo and as an Orisha, while others consider him only as an Orisha. Shango is believed to have dominion over natural phenomena like thunder and lightning, fire, and drumming. Often depicted wielding a double-headed axe, Shango's weapon symbolizes his power over lightning. He is also depicted wearing garments in the colors of red and white. Shango is a passionate and dynamic deity associated with male virility and masculinity. He fiercely protects his followers and those who seek his help in cases of injustice.

Shango is believed to aid those he protects in overcoming their challenges and obstacles, providing them with the strength and vitality to succeed. Certain stones, such as the thunder stone, flint, chert, and obsidian, are associated with Shango. Offerings to Shango include red wine, rum, tobacco, red and white candles, roasted yams or cornmeal, red peppers, bitter cola, porridge, okra, roosters, guinea hens, palm oil, bananas, water, incense, and candles. One taboo with Shango is offering him Adin Dudu or Black Palm Kernel oil.

YEMAYA

The Orisha Yemaya, also spelled Yemanja, is a popular deity in Yoruba culture. She is the ruler of the saltwater, ocean surface, and waves. Yemaya is often depicted as a mermaid and represents motherhood. She is also believed to be the mother of all fish. While Yemaya governs the visible surface of the ocean, Olokun rules the invisible, dark depths of the ocean. It is believed that wherever the sun's light can penetrate within the ocean, Yemaya has dominion, and wherever the sun's light cannot penetrate, Olokun has authority. Yemaya is known for her calming and nurturing energy, which helps to balance the energies of Olokun. However, if she becomes angered, she can be violent and unforgiving. Yemaya is often called upon for guidance, comfort, and protection. She is associated with fertility and is often invoked by women who are trying to conceive. Her colors are blue, white, and clear, and some stones associated with her include Lapis Lazuli, coral, pearls, all seashells, aquamarine, and azurite. Offerings to Yemaya often include white and blue flowers, melons, molasses, seashells, blue and white candles, jewelry, honey, coconut, and various types of seafood, fish, and pigeons, cowrie shells.

YEWA

Yewa, also known as Ayaba, is a mysterious Orisha. Whereas Oya, her sister, rules over the barrier between life and death and is present at the gates of the cemetery, Yewa is very much associated with the earth and the ground, as the dead are buried there. She resides inside the cemetery. Both Oya and Yewa ensure that the barriers of life and death are kept separate. The barrier between these two worlds may be slightly lifted at certain times of the year so humanity can celebrate and pay tribute to those who have died, and the dead can also participate in the celebrations. However, this belief is limited by the community, and some Orisha practitioners may not hold this view. Yewa is often associated with beauty and the mysteries of death, as she is said to rule over the decomposition of corpses. Offerings given to her include cowrie shells, flowers, water, incense, candles, pigeons, and female goats.

CHAPTER 4

THE CONCEPT
OF ATUNWA

IN PRIOR CHAPTERS, we spoke about the sacred connection that we have with nature. In this chapter, we will talk about our connection to the cycle of life, death and rebirth. The Yoruba call this process Atunwa. The concept of Atunwa is like the idea of reincarnation in some ways, but differs in other ways. In Atunwa, unlike in reincarnation, there are two worlds that a soul (Emi) can be reborn into, as in reincarnation, it is often believed that the soul can only be reborn into the physical world. In Atunwa, however, the soul or ''emi'' often transitions back and forth from the physical-material world to the spiritual world, and these transitions are seen as separate.

The first of these two worlds is the physical world, and the second world is heaven or the world of spirit. The first principle of Atunwa is that when a soul leaves a body at death in the physical world, it may stay in the physical world for a time afterwards, but inevitably returns to the world of the spirit, commonly called Orun. At this point, the spirit may decide to return to the earth as another person in a different body. Another unique aspect of Atunwa is the idea that when a person dies, their spirit is reborn in a new body that is a part of the same family lineage. Whereas in reincarnation, this distinction is not made. The understanding of Atunwa originates from the worldview that life is cyclical and that everything in the universe is interconnected. The Yoruba also believe rebirth is not automatic. Instead, it is believed that the spirit of the deceased must undergo a series of purification rituals and ceremonies in the afterlife before it can be reborn again in the physical world. These rituals are intended to cleanse the spirit of any impurities. The word Atunwa originates from the Yoruba word, which means "again to give birth".

There are several ways in which Atunwa can happen. One way this happens is called *iPadawaye,* which means the ancestor has returned. When children are born, they are taken to an Ifa Priest called a Babalawo to determine which ancestor has reincarnated as the child. The name of the child is often derived from the ancestor's name in this way. This type of rebirth is by far the most common for all of us. We often reincarnate many times over. It is also believed that we reincarnate within our same family line, so traditionally, when a child is born into the world, it is common for the Babalawo to determine which ancestor that child was in their prior life within their family lineage.

Another kind of Atunwa is *Akudaya*. This type of rebirth is technically not rebirth, but is where a soul is stuck here on earth and unable to move forward to heaven. This soul continues to live here on earth (*aye*) in spirit form to gain merit due to not completing their prior life or due to negative actions during their prior life. These spirits may continue to wander around on the Earth for a time. They may serve to protect, help, and guide their living family members. They may do this to regain merit, sufficient *ase* to enter orun (heaven). These spirits tend to live on Earth as *Iwin* "ghost" if they have no living family, or could be in the process of becoming an Egun (ancestor) if, in fact, they do have living descendants still on earth. Once they finish up with their unfinished business on earth from their prior life, it is believed the portal will open for them to return to heaven, and at that point, they will become a part of the egun, the ancestral dead. Sometimes these earthly spirits will appear as if they have a body and then vanish once their real name is revealed. The last category of Atunwa is known as *Abiku*.

Yes, such stories exist, often associated with specific circumstances. One scenario involves punishment for displaying poor character during their human life. Another could result from improper burial and the failure to perform necessary funeral rites. One crucial aspect of the funeral rite is the presence of a Babalawo, who conducts divination in the deceased's name to determine the required sacrifices for a smooth transition to the afterlife, preventing them from becoming stuck in the world of the living. The cautionary tale below illustrates the significance of proper burial rites:

In a distant village, there were two brothers, one older and one younger, both skilled hunters whose arrows always found their mark. One day, the village chief announced a hunting competition to determine the best hunter. Both brothers competed, and the younger brother emerged victorious, earning praise and rewards from the villagers. However, on their way home, the elder brother, consumed by greed, murdered his younger brother to claim his share of the reward.

Several years later, their mother, while walking in the forest, stumbled upon her younger son's remains, which had become entwined with moss. Crying, she gathered the bones and brought them home. The following day, the mother sought counsel from both the Babalawo and the chief. The Babalawo (Ifa Priest), after consulting the Ifa Oracle, told the mother that they must offer a sacrifice at the place where she found the bones and perform a proper burial rite. The following morning, both the Babalawo and the mother took the sacrifice to this location. That night, an ancestor appeared to the mother in a dream, revealing the truth of the elder broth-

er's crime and that the soul of the younger brother, due to an improper burial, had partially become part of the moss. The proper burial rites were then completed, and the chief, upon hearing this case, brought it to the King.

After hearing testimony from all parties, the King decreed that the elder brother should be executed for his crime. The mother, upon hearing this, pleaded with the King to spare her older son's life. Moved by her plea, the King decided to show mercy and instead banished the older son from the city. With justice served and the proper funerary rites performed, the spirit of the younger brother found peace. Six months later, the mother became pregnant again, and it was discovered that the soul of the younger son was to be reborn, finally released from the tragic event that had occurred in his prior life.

The connection between the fungus and the deceased son was evident, symbolizing his soul's presence due to the absence of funeral rites. In Yoruba tradition, timely offerings and prayers upon death ensure a smooth transition to the next stage.

WHO ARE THE ABIKU?

Abiku, also known as Ogbanje in some parts of Nigeria, refers to a type of child believed to be born with a predestined mission to die and return. The term Abiku comes from the Yoruba words "Abo" meaning predestined, and "Iku, " meaning death. The belief in Abiku is a spiritual phenomenon beyond human understanding and is a common cultural belief amongst the Yoruba. Some traditional Yoruba practices include giving the child a special name or performing certain rituals, such as tattooing, to mark the child's body to prevent the child from dying.

It has also been said that sometimes a soul may enter the physical world from heaven through the birth process just to get to earth, but once here, discards the physical body due to not needing it to achieve the destiny they chose in heaven. Instead, they choose to continue to live on earth and fulfill their destiny in spirit form rather than in physical form. It is said that the divinities will not let a soul back into heaven until its tasks in the world are finished, even if they are in spirit form and continue to exist on earth in this form without a physical presence.

Sometimes, a spirit can accumulate Ase or spiritual energy by helping or guiding their family members here on earth to fulfill their purpose if they did not fulfill it when they were alive previously. Sometimes these spirits will either stay on the earth after they have died, called Akudaya, or may come back to the earth in a future time as an Abiku. It may also be true that perhaps some of these souls die prematurely due to simply not needing a lot of time to accomplish their mission in the world and immediately return to heaven after accomplishing what they needed to do on earth. A third reason for the existence of Abiku spirits may be that when the soul decided to come to earth, the soul did not pick the right Ori-inu (spiritual head) to support them. In this case the things mentioned above may be done such as giving the child a special name or performing certain rituals, such as tattooing, to mark the child's body to prevent the child from dying may be performed as an attempt to save the child from dying. Often these things are done while a child is severely ill or overcame a situation where the child could have died to protect the child and prevent further harm or possible death from taking the child sooner than expected.

In conclusion, the belief in Abiku serves as a reminder of the impermanence of life and that we will all one day die. It reminds us that we should not take life for granted but instead consider every day we are alive as a miracle.

Go to a local cemetery and just sit there and contemplate your own mortality. Bring a notebook and write in it two columns. The one column represents all the things that matter in your life. The other column represents all the things one stresses over in life that, in the larger picture, are not as important. In today's world, especially in the Western part, materialism has become the new religion. We are taught to live for today and not prepare for tomorrow. It is always important to realize that when we all die, our bones will become a part of the earth. It is often difficult to distinguish rich from poor in a cemetery beside a slightly larger tombstone. One cannot distinguish race either; these are important points to keep in mind when dealing with people in the living. If they are relevant in death, perhaps they are relevant as well while being alive.

Lastly, ask yourself what it is that you desire to do to bring meaning to your life and others before you die? What are some things you desire to accomplish? What are some things you need to stop doing that are a waste of your life? You may need to repeat this activity multiple times or over several days. Recognizing that we are all going to die is crucial to our own spiritual development. The beautiful thing about the Orisha/ Yoruba spirituality, however, is the fact that we believe that death is never the end and that our relationships with the ones we love, whom we have lost, are in fact still with us even after they have passed. Life is also considered a huge blessing to learn and grow. Life is not meant to be easy, and the lessons we learn in life help us grow.

* * *

CHAPTER 5
HONORING THE ANCESTORS

IN THE YORUBA TRADITION, the family consists not just of the living members but also the deceased members, who are continually honored and not forgotten by the living members. The ancestors are believed to be a vital link between the physical and spiritual worlds, acting as intermediaries who help to guide and assist the living throughout their lives. Orisha practitioners in Yoruba land and in the diaspora use the words Egun and Egungun to refer to the spirits of the deceased family members who continue to exist in the spiritual realm after death. However, there are some key differences between the two concepts that are important to recognize.

Egun generally refers to the individual ancestral spirits of a particular family, such as a specific ancestor who has passed away. Egun is believed to have a deep connection to their living descendants and to play a role in their welfare, protection, and guidance. Family members may offer prayers, libations, and other offerings to honor their Egun, with the intention of strengthening their connection and receiving their blessings. Honoring our Egun is of the utmost importance in Yoruba culture. On the other hand, Egungun refers to a collective ancestral energy that includes all deceased family members from multiple generations. It is believed that this collective energy is manifested as an Orisha, also known as Egungun, that serves as a vital connection between the physical and spiritual worlds. Egungun is believed to be one of the sons of the Orisha Oya and is thought to have a powerful healing influence on humanity. Offerings are made to this Orisha to invoke the blessings and protection of all ancestors, especially during public celebrations where ancestors are honored by all members of a village or a town, like in the Egungun Masquerade.

THE EGUNGUN MASQUERADE

The Egungun Masquerade takes place once a year in the month of June. It is a colorful and vibrant celebration where members of the community come together to honor Egungun. During the festival, masked performers dressed in elaborate costumes of many different colors represent the variety of diverse ancestors. These dancers are known as the 'Alagbe'. They are trained individuals who have been initiated into the cult of the Egungun and have the knowledge and authority to wear the Egungun costume, dance, and perform the rituals. The Alagbe are considered the representatives of the Egungun and are believed to possess the spiritual power of the ancestors. As the sacred dancers move through the streets, accompanied by drumming and dancing, people will get out of their way and avoid coming near them or touching them.

The Egungun Masquerade is celebrated by the Yoruba for various reasons, including to honor and show respect to ancestors, seek their blessings, and maintain the spiritual and cultural identity of the community. The festival also serves as a time for community bonding and strengthening family ties, as it is a time when family members come together to honor their ancestors and celebrate their cultural heritage. The Egungun Masquerade is a deeply spiritual and symbolic celebration, and it is believed that the spirits of the ancestors are present during the festival. The performers who take part in the celebration are believed to act as the messengers of the ancestors. The story of how the Egungun Masquerade began starts with a disagreement between two brothers, Egungun and Oro, and the story goes as follows:

There were two brothers, Egungun and Oro. They both harbored a shared desire to descend to Earth from Orun (heaven) together, seeking to amplify their wealth. Prior to their earthly venture, both siblings sought counsel from Orunmila, consulting Ifa for guidance and receiving the Odu: **Ojuani Osa**. *Orunmila's counsel emphasized that wealth awaited them if they shared their blessings with devotees upon reaching Earth.*

Eager to realize their aspirations, Egungun took the initiative, descending to Earth while Oro remained in the heavens. Oro, trusting in his brother's promise, implored Egungun to return once the coast was clear. Egungun, agreeing to the plan, arrived on Earth and, when queried by villagers, declared his mission to aid those in need. Generosity defined Egungun's actions, leading to multiplied wealth and offerings on specified days. His benevolence garnered immediate respect from both villagers and powerful kings, accompanied by numerous gifts. Simultaneously, Oro, observing his brother's festivities from heaven, was met with disappointment as Egungun ignored his calls. Enraged by the broken promise, Oro descended after sunset, shrouding the sky in darkness. Intent on confronting his brother, Oro chased Egungun, inciting fear among the villagers who sought refuge in their homes. Facing the dispute, Egungun and wise village elders approached Oro. Acknowledging his abilities, Oro, fueled by anger, demanded justice for the broken promise.

A resolution emerged as Egungun, recognizing the injustice, agreed to honor Oro by limiting his celebrations to daylight. Oro, in turn, would be celebrated after sunset when darkness enveloped the sky. The wise elders celebrated Oro as a symbol of justice and fairness, but would only celebrate him at night. When the sun arose the following morning, Oro retreated into the forest, cementing his role as the patron of justice in the world.

* * *

Some Yoruba see Oro as a historical king who ruled over a vast kingdom. He was known for his wisdom and just rule, and his people loved and respected him greatly. However, one day, Oro disappeared mysteriously, and his people were left to wonder where he had gone. After a long search, it was discovered that Oro had been transformed into a spirit and had gone to live in the spirit world. He was no longer visible to mortals, but he continued to watch over his people and protect them from harm. Over time, the cult of Oro emerged, and it became a powerful force in Yoruba society. The members of the Oro cult were believed to be the only ones who had access to Oro and could communicate with him directly.

The Egungun, on the other hand, were believed to be the spirits of ancestors who had passed on to the spirit world. They were also considered to be powerful protectors of their descendants and were venerated in Yoruba society. However, the relationship between Oro and Egungun was not always peaceful. In fact, there was a long-standing feud between the two groups that dated back centuries. Oro is primarily associated with the forest and hunting, as well as with justice, just as Egungun is associated with the ancestors. Oro is also associated with Egbe, who are referred to as heavenly mates, and he is also associated with the ancestors to a lesser extent than his brother. Oro is the Orisha that brings spiritual justice on behalf of the ancestors and the Egbe. Oro is commonly depicted wearing animal skins and carrying hunting weapons.

The Oro festival is a major cultural event in many regions of Nigeria among the Yoruba. The festival often occurs once a year and is marked by the performance of traditional music, dance, and the wearing of elaborate costumes. The Oro rituals are performed during the festival at night in secret. Oro is often depicted as a masked figure during the festival, with only initiated members of the community being allowed to participate and be part of the festival. Everyone else, including women, foreigners, and children, must stay inside the home once night falls. Many Yoruba people see the Oro Festival to ward off evil, protect the community, and bring justice; however, it is important to note that the Oro festival has been controversial in some regions due to its secrecy and exclusionary nature. There have been concerns about its potential to be used for political and social control, especially from people of certain other religions who desire to cast a negative image on the Yoruba-Orisha indigenous faith.

Egungun, on the other hand, is directly associated with the ancestors and the specific spirits of the dead, as mentioned above. Egungun is also a protector of the community. Egungun rituals are mostly public and involve elaborate costumes, dance, and performances, just like the Oro Festival. The difference is that the Egungun Masquerade takes place during the day, and everyone, including foreigners, is welcome to attend the Egungun Masquerade Festival. Despite their differences, Oro and Egungun are closely related because both are associated with the world of the dead, but both are never to be honored together.

THE DISTINCTION BETWEEN EGUN AND IWIN

The term Iwin means ghost. These are spirits that are not considered ancestors or Egbe, or heavenly mates, which we will get into later. A spouse, a friend, or an adoptive parent, a biological brother or sister who has passed away, may not be considered Egun but may be Egbe. There are some differences in opinions on who qualifies as Egun, but what I am saying here is the consensus for the most part. Our Egun, or ancestors, are often defined as those people who have not only direct blood ties with us but also are responsible for us being born. Both these qualifications are often met with those who are categorized as Egun. Both Egun and Egbe can have a direct responsibility for us being born into the world, but only Egun can have direct blood and genetic ties with that as well. We often honor our Egun at an Egun shrine located within our home or outside near it. Both Egbe and Egun are honored equally but separately. The Egun shrine symbolizes all your Egun for the last nine generations, not just one. It is this ancestral consciousness you are honoring with the shrine, not a particular ancestor. Honoring ancestors is always a personal choice. Honoring non-Egun at an Egun shrine or someone else's ancestors at your Egun shrine should be considered taboo. One can have a separate shrine to honor Egbe and another for those spirits that do not fall into either Egun or Egbe but are called Iwin, but they should all be honored at separate shrines. They should be honored separately but equally. A common practice in the Diaspora is to honor one's Egbe using the Boveda or the "white table" in Spanish, and one's ancestors with the ancestral shrine. We will talk about the Boveda in the next chapter.

Honoring Egun

We may also choose not to honor certain ancestors who may be violent or harmful to us, or who do not support us, even if they are blood relatives. We always have a choice not to honor a particular ancestor if we choose not to do so, but one should consider consulting IFA on the matter to ensure the spirit is truly not supportive. Honoring Egun is about honoring the ancestral connection we have to our own consciousness. Any spirit, blood-related or not, that intends harm upon us, it is our choice to decide whether to recognize them. Just as in life, we may want to distance ourselves from harmful people, the same goes for spirits that do not have our highest good at heart. We normally can choose not to honor these spirits. However, if one is unsure whether one should honor a particular ancestor, one should always consult IFA through a Babalawo so one can know for certain if this ancestor should be honored.

It is often believed that one or two ancestors within your mother's or father's line are your guardian ancestors. These ancestors are the most active ancestors, and they look out for you while you're on earth. Also, the other ancestors communicate with these ancestors, who in turn communicate with you. It is often told by IFA who the person's main ancestors are during an IFA consultation. Often, the Priest or Priestess will provide this information to the person prior to their initiation. Here is an example to illustrate what I mean by one of my clients' consultations. IFA determined for him that it was his third great-grandfather on his father's side and his 2nd great-grandmother on his mother's side who are the two most active ancestors that support him. These two ancestors would be considered his guardian ancestors because they are the most active in supporting him.

SHOULD I HONOR MY BABALÁWO'S ANCESTORS, MY SPIRITUAL TEACHER'S ANCESTORS, OR BOTH IN THE IFÁ, ORISHA TRADITION?

It is often said in some religious houses, particularly in the diaspora, that practitioners must honor the ancestors of the Babalawo or the house's priest or priestess as *Egun*. In my view, however, religious parents or godparents hold spiritual titles within the tradition, but they are not the same as one's actual blood ancestors. The so-called "ancestors of the spiritual house" may be respected and acknowledged, but they should not be honored in the same way as one's blood ancestors unless *Ifa* specifically permits it. For this reason, I would never advise my students to honor my ancestors. Each person has the responsibility to honor their own lineage, not the ancestors of someone else.

Humans, due to their physical bodies, experience a reduced state of awareness compared to the state of consciousness we have when outside the body. Our awareness is primarily focused on the present reality of our current time and place, which we refer to as the present moment. While awake, we can only perceive what is happening here and now, unable to simultaneously experience events in different places. This limitation, though it may seem restrictive, serves as a blessing. It allows us to concentrate on the present, aiding us in working towards our destiny. Despite the challenges it presents, this focus proves beneficial. In stark contrast, when the spirit departs from the body at death, it transitions from a contracted state of awareness to an expanded one. This expanded awareness permits the spirit to exist in multiple places and dimensions at once, enabling it to support and guide those on Earth. However, there are exceptions to this rule. During sleep or when receiving intuitive messages from the spirit world, we can catch glimpses of this expanded consciousness or out-of-body awareness.

The limitations imposed by our physical bodies, which I refer to as the contracted state of awareness, are crucial for our spiritual growth and development. This necessity for spirits to return and be reborn in new bodies to re-experience this contracted state underlines its importance. For a spiritual being to achieve growth, it must journey through both contracted and expanded states of awareness. This concept is known as the Dual States of Awareness, which encompasses two primary states of human consciousness: the Contracted State of Awareness and the Expanded State of Awareness.

- **Esu. Eshu, Elegua** - *acts as an intermediary between heaven and earth. He takes the sacrifice called ebò for both the living and the dead and directs it to where it needs to go.*
- **Oya** - *Egungun is considered a son of the Orisha Oya. Oya protects all the dead, including both the Iwin or Ghosts and ancestors. Oya is also the keeper of the cemetery and the gatekeeper to the realm of the ancestors. She is associated with change, transformation, and the mysteries of life and death.*
- **Obaluaye, Sopona**: *Orisha of sickness and health, Obaluaye is also known as the keeper of the Egun. He is associated with the earth and the secrets of life and death.*
- **Oshun**: *Orisha of the rivers and streams, Osun is also associated with fertility, love, and healing. She is often invoked during ceremonies honoring the ancestors.*
- **Yewa**: *Orisha of the cemetery, whereas Oya rules the gates and the boundaries of the cemetery, Yewa is associated with the cemetery itself. Yewa is associated with beauty, purity, and the mysteries of life and death.*
- **Orunmila**: *Orisha of wisdom and divination, Orunmila is believed to have a close relationship with the ancestors. He is often consulted during divination for help and guidance from both the living and the dead on earth as well as in heaven.*
- **Obatala**: *is often depicted as the father of all Orishas and is associated with the color white, which represents purity and the creative force of the universe. Obatala is also associated with coolness, calmness, and tranquility, and is often invoked for healing, peace, and spiritual guidance.*

* * *

Finally it can be said that,, in Yoruba philosophy, honoring the ancestors is ultimately an act of remembering who we are and where we come from. The living, the dead, and the unborn exist in a continuous relationship, bound by responsibility, consciousness, and moral order. By honoring Egun with clarity and discernment, we affirm the sacred balance between lineage and choice, tradition and accountability. In doing so, we are reminded that spiritual growth is not found in confusion or excess, but in right relationship with our ancestors, our community, and our own inner awareness.

CHAPTER 6
AT THE ANCESTORS' SHRINE

IT IS SAID that when we give offerings to Egun, this gives our ancestors the strength to support, protect, and bless us in our lives. We went over some of the topics and understanding of the ancestors in the prior chapter. In this chapter, we will discuss further how to honor your ancestors. Understanding the origins of this practice could partly be explained by the following legend.

*A son was once faced with a tragic loss when his father accidentally fell to his death during a hunting trip. Overwhelmed by grief, the son distanced himself from the site and left his father there without giving him a proper burial. For several years, the son encountered numerous hardships as the years unfolded. Seeking answers, he consulted a knowledgeable Babalawo who, through the guidance of IFA, casted the Odu: **Oyeku Meji**. The Babalawo advised the son to return to the hunting grounds and properly bury his father. Following the Babalawo's counsel, the son retrieved his father's bones at the site. By this time, the animals had scattered many of the bones.*

The son managed to collect most of them, tied them together with a red cloth, and brought them to the Babalawo. The Babalawo then conducted

IFA-prescribed sacrifices and helped the son bury the father near the son's home, creating a sacred space by a grove of trees. This Babalawo then gave the son a stick adorned with nine differently colored cloths. The son was instructed to use it for communication with both his and his father's ancestors, tapping the ground nine times. Embracing this ritual, the Babalawo guided the son in erecting a shrine. This sacred space became a focal point for the son and his descendants to honor their ancestors, seek guidance, and offer thanks. The son, following these practices, ascended to a position of importance, advising the king and Chiefs, accumulating wealth, and witnessing prosperity for nine generations of his descendants.

* * *

This story seems to illustrate the important power our ancestors have within our lives and why we should always honor them. It is often said that if someone is in trouble and this is not communicated to the ancestors, they may not be aware of it, and therefore, they may not know they need to intervene. The second thing the story teaches us is the importance of sacrifice. Sacrifice plays a crucial role in our religion and the life of the traditional Yoruba. The story also teaches us why we use both the **Atori Sticks** and the **Pagugu** when honoring our ancestors.

Part of the **Isan-Egungun** consists of 9 sticks wrapped in a red cloth commonly called the Atori Sticks. These Atori sticks are meant to represent the bones of the ancestors. The number 9 is sacred to the Orisha Oya, and 9 also represents the 9 generations of ancestors we are meant to honor. Atori sticks are made from a sacred wood and given through a ceremonial process. They are often used as a focal point to invoke the spirits of the ancestors, both in the personal Egun shrine and are often used during Egungun ceremonies, where they will sometimes be displayed on top of the heads of the covered dancers referred to as the Alagba Egungun, who are believed to be possessed by the spirits of the ancestors during the dance.

The Atori sticks are used as a conduit for the spirits to possess these dancers. Yoruba spiritual practitioners will often perform various sacrifices to their ancestors by using the Atori sticks as the focal point for their rituals as well.

Another element that is important in ancestor devotion is the *Pagugu,* commonly called the Ancestors' staff or an Egun walking Stick. The *Pagugu* is a stick about 4 to 6 ft. tall made from the same sacred wood as the Atori is made from, and is decorated with various pieces of colorful clothes tied around it. Traditionally, there were nine cloths, each a different color. Nine again is the number of the Orisha Oya and traditionally represents the diversity of ancestors within someone's lineage. We will often tap the ground nine times with the Pagugu in honoring our ancestors to wake the ancestors and invoke them.

ADDITIONAL ITEMS COMMONLY FOUND IN AN
EGUN SHRINE

A cross or other unique cultural symbols that were important to your ancestors when they were alive. I will often display a cross on my ancestors' shrine. The first reason is that it represents the crossroads between the spirit world and the physical world, and secondly, it serves as a representation to the numerous ancestors in my gene pool who identified as Christians. The cross is a good example of a symbol that can mean one thing for one group of people and another thing for a different group. It is okay to utilize symbols from other religions on your ancestor's shrine without being a part of that religion. I will often have a sacred herb bundle wrapped up in leather, commonly referred to as a "medicine bundle," as well as on my ancestor's shrine to represent my native Indigenous American ancestors.

You may also desire to use or may see in use an **Egun Tile;** the tile is more common in the diaspora than in Africa. Traditionally, the tile would have been constructed with the dirt from the graves or the dirt from the land where a person's ancestors were laid to rest. The dirt would be mixed with clay and baked. Today, however, especially in the diaspora, the tile is made of terracotta clay and is consecrated by a Babalawo or Iyanifa. In the diaspora, the tile often symbolizes the connection to the motherland, Africa, as well as the ground where all of humanity will one day lie to rest. The dirt in Nigeria has a reddish/ brown terracotta coloration. There is a myth that some of the enslaved Africans may have brought some of the dirt from their homeland with them to the Caribbean across the Atlantic, and from this dirt and the dirt and clay of the new world, created a tile that connected them to their ancestors in the motherland.

Ere Egun, which are used in a variety of religious ceremonies and rituals in Yoruba culture. They are often adorned with brightly colored fabrics, beads, and other decorative materials, and are a visual representation of the spirits of the ancestors in some regions, and in other regions, these figures are believed to be inhabited by the spirits of the ancestors. It is common to see photos of someone's ancestors on their shrine. It is important that when using photographs on any spiritual altar honoring the dead, the photographs only contain an image of the deceased, and they don't contain any images of living family members that have not passed on.

OTHER IMPORTANT THINGS TO INCLUDE

A white candle, I will often use battery-powered candles because they pose less of a risk of burning. There is often a glass of water or several glasses of other offerings or drinks, and sometimes a bowl with various foods. The ancestor shrine is traditionally located on the ground in a corner near a wall, if it is in the home, but sometimes you will see them outside the house as well.

BUILDING A PLACE TO HONOR YOUR ANCESTORS

I am under the belief that everyone has access to their ancestors and can construct an ancestral shrine by themselves without needing religious consecration, except for the various tools we discussed above. Clear and purify the space that you will be using to set up your ancestors' shrine or Boveda. I recommend using some incense, or you can use sage or a combination of these things to clean the space. With the incense or herbs you decide to use. You will first light them using a match or a flame, and with a feather or your own hands, gently flame some of the smoke towards the area you desire to clean. In doing this, you will recite the following prayer either in English or Yoruba or whichever one you feel most comfortable with.

PRAYER FOR REMOVING
NEGATIVE ENERGY

Mo pe oruko Olodumare lati nu
I call upon the name of the Almighty.
aaye yi kuro ki o si ko gbogbo
to cleanse this place and agbara buburu kuro.
Remove all evil forces. Mo juba Olorun,
I give respect to Olodumare
Mo juba Eggun
I give respect to my ancestors.
Mo juba Orisha
I give respect to the Orishas.
Ase, may this prayer be sealed!

***

Following the prayer and incense, I will normally let the incense burn and go out on its own and will leave it in the spot I am cleansing, either in a bowl or in some container. The next thing I will do is open the window to clear out all the energies so the smoke can carry the energy out. After this, I will use some water and a branch with leaves on it and sprinkle water into the area. I am cleansing using the branch or my fingers. I often enjoy adding some oils to the water, my favorite being lavender or rose, but you can choose to do this or not do this. Plain water works. While doing this, I suggest you recite the prayer below called the Omi Tutu:

THE OMI TUTU PRAYER

You will need a small bowl of water for this prayer.

Dab your fingers or a branch in the water and let it drop on the **GROUND,** then recite the verses below:

Omi Tutu, Omi Tutu: Cool water, fresh Water
Omi Tutu, Omi Tutu: Cool water, fresh Water
Omi Tutu, Omi Tutu: Cool water, fresh Water

Again, dab your fingers or a branch in the water and let it drop on the **GROUND,** then recite the verse below:

Omi Tutu: Cool water, fresh Water
Ile Tutu: Refresh the house

Again, dab your fingers or a branch in the water and let it drop on the **GROUND,** then recite the verse below:

Omi Tutu: Cool water, fresh Water
Ona Tutu: Refresh my roads

Again, dab your fingers or a branch in the water and let it drop on the **GROUND,** then recite the verse below:

Omi Tutu: Cool water, fresh Water
Egun Tutu: Refresh the ancestors
Mojuba Olodumare: I give praise to Olodumare
Mojuba Orishas: I give praise to the Orishas.
Mojuba Iya tobi Mi: I praise my mother.
Mojuba Baba tobi mi: I praise my father.
Mojuba Eggun: I praise the ancestors.
Ase, may this prayer be sealed!

* * *

ONCE THE ABOVE IS COMPLETED,
YOU CAN BEGIN SETTING UP YOUR ANCESTOR SHRINE

Suppose you are setting up your ancestor shrine within the home. The first thing you should do is locate a corner of the room that is private, perhaps a place that will acquire the least amount of traffic, either from people or pets. Find the space before doing the cleansing space ritual described above.

Gather your materials: decide what you want to put on your ancestors' shrine. You may want to start with a simple setup at first, which would include some photos or an item that belonged to your ancestors, a white candle, a cup to give your ancestors a drink offering, and a plate to give them food offerings. Sometimes the ancestors' shrine will have two cups, one for various offerings like coffee or alcohol, and another for water that is always available and filled. Some flowers, a live plant or some incense may be included as well. If you have Atari Sticks, include them. It is common to keep them in a tureen.

Preparation: If the shrine is located inside rather than outside, it should be in a corner of the house where the two walls meet and on the floor.

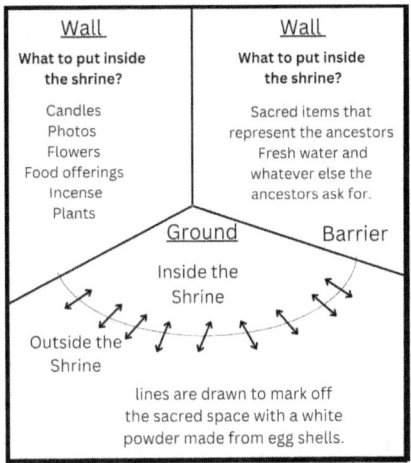

Make sure you clean all the dust and debris from the area prior to setting up your shrine. Many people will draw a round line on the ground from one wall to the other wall enclosing the corner in the center, which is the area that the ancestors' shrine will be in. If you decide to draw the line, you will want to draw it with a white chalk called cascarilla powder, which is traditionally made from ground-up eggshells. You could also use cornmeal, flour, or even sugar to draw the line; however, don't use salt. After this, you will draw 9 separate little lines through the circle to make it look like a sun with 9 separate rays, as shown in the image above. The inside of this circle represents your ancestors' space, and the outside represents everything else.

WHAT IS SACRED SPACE?

Sacred space refers to a place that is considered holy or imbued with spiritual power, while profane space is simply the ordinary physical world. Once you draw the barrier that divides the sacred space of the ancestors' shrine from the profane space of the rest of the world, it is crucial that you respect this space as no longer a part of the ordinary world but a place for the ancestors, as if it were their home, because it is where they come to visit you. If you desire to offer something to them or retrieve something from within the space, you should ask them first. How you do this is to obtain 4 cowrie shells and go to the section of this book on Obi Divination to learn more about how to communicate with your ancestors.

Opening the Shrine

To do this, you will tap the floor nine times with your ancestor's stick, the *Pagugu* stick. You will then light a candle and place it within the shrine, and within the circular line you drew as the barrier of the shrine, dividing your ancestor's space from your space or the space of other things or people. You can use a small battery-operated candle or light, which is often less dangerous if you desire to do so. The purpose of this is to provide light and illumination to the spiritual energies you are honoring and to invite them into the space. Candles or lamps can also be used to focus the practitioner's attention and intentions while in meditation, prayer, or while honoring their ancestors. Finally, you will pour a fresh glass of clear water for your ancestors and put it inside the shrine with the light. Water is a powerful symbol of purification. Water is often used to cleanse oneself before engaging in spiritual practices, and it is also used to symbolically cleanse the space where the spiritual practice will take place. Water is also used in offerings to spirits, as a way of showing respect and offering something pure and refreshing.

This is essentially a basic ancestor shrine; water and light are the two most important elements needed in building a basic shrine, as well as simply offering up the space for your ancestors within your home or place of residence. You will also need your *Pagugu* stick as mentioned above. It is important to note that this space is dedicated to your ancestors and is, in turn, their space. Using the *Pagugu* stick is the equivalent of knocking on the door and asking them to invite you into their space.

Finally, you can recite a prayer or talk to them like you would a living person while sitting in front of the shrine. The most important thing is to be present and to dedicate the time sitting with your ancestors with them. This means shutting out all the other things in your life and simply being present and listening to that inner voice that guides us all. If you decide to give another offering of food and drink to your ancestors, you can choose to do this at this time if you feel moved to do so. The most basic offering is a glass of water and a white candle, unless they are asking for other things as well.

Communication with your ancestors begins by speaking with them as if they were present and asking them for their guidance and blessings. As you spend more time at your shrine, you will develop the intuition of knowing what they want or are saying.

You will be able to tap into your ancestral matrix, which will facilitate your communication with them, but this will take time and dedication by making time frequently to honor them. We often use divination as a tool to check if our intuition is correct.

For this, you will need 4 cowrie shells. Once you have acquired them, read the section of the book on obi divination, which will teach you how to ask questions to ensure that your intuition is correct.

CLOSING THE SHRINE

When you are finished, thank your ancestors for their presence and guidance. Extinguish the candles; one should not blow out candles but instead snuff them out using some water or an object. If they are battery-operated candles, you can choose to leave them on. This is totally up to you. I always recommend, however, that real candles get snuffed out when left unattended due to the potential for a fire. Finally, you can choose to cover the shrine with a white cloth to prevent dust and debris from falling. This is again up to you. I will normally put a white cloth over some of the glasses or food offerings, as well as my Atori sticks, and any offerings made, but again, this is totally up to your preferences.

Finally, it is important to maintain the shrine: Clean and maintain the shrine regularly. Dedicating yourself to your ancestors' shrine should be done at least once a week to keep the connection with your ancestors strong.

WHY DO WE CALL FORTH OUR ANCESTORS TO SUPPORT US?

When we call forth our ancestors, we are calling forth all the ancestors who support us. We are calling all the people who are responsible for our birth, all the way back to the beginning of time. We are remembering them and letting them know that we acknowledge their sacrifices for us to be here. This ancestral consciousness is a part of our DNA and what we inherited from those who lived before us. It is believed that because we have this connection, we can connect with them. This connection goes back to the primordial creation and the first human. Regardless of race or culture or class, we all have way more biological similarities than differences, and we all come from the same place. This is why we honor our ancestors.

WHAT SHOULD I GIVE TO MY ANCESTORS?

Some offerings to the ancestors include White Flowers, white candle, water, Kola nuts, white porridge with sugar and milk, black beans, various fruits including green bananas, Coffee, Alcoholic Beverages are some things one can offer to their ancestors. Including some of the things they may have eaten when they were alive.

Note: Sometimes you will hear the ancestors being called "Egun Baba" for the male ancestors on our father's side and "Egun Iya" for the female ancestors on our mother's side. These terms are often used to call upon the souls of our direct ancestors, such as the souls of our parents and grandparents on the mother's and father's sides.

Regional and National Egun

Regional and national Egun are often referred to as *Egun Agbegbe.* These ancestors are normally honored by the community as a whole, and their shrines are sometimes put in public places in the city or town. These ancestors may be considered national or local heroes, Kings, and other people who have made an impact on the community. Many Yoruba people consider Odùdúwà as the first spiritual ancestor who unites all the Yoruba people. Often, it is common for the direct descendants of these ancestors to take care of the public communal shrine, which is the shrine located in the public square or place within the city.

These public shrines are often taken care of by the blood descendants of the Eguns themselves or someone who is elected to the position if a descendant is not present. This position of caring for these public shrines is often considered an honorable public service position, which would include receiving donations from people and being compensated financially by the state for this duty of caring for the shrines.

On the Topic of Prayer

The word Oriki is often used generically within the Yoruba spiritual tradition to refer to prayer. Oriki translates as a poem or poetry. It is traditional for prayers to be written and recited in the Yoruba language. It is said that the Orishas can understand all languages, so if you don't know Yoruba, that is fine. However, it is often traditional for the Yoruba language to be used in ceremonies, rituals, prayers, and other forms of devotion in the Orisha tradition. This is even true in many of the diaspora traditions where a dialect of Yoruba is still used for religious purposes, such as in Cuba.

There are several different classes of prayers within the Orisha tradition. Here is a list of some of the different types of prayers:

- **Oriki-Adura**: *These are often considered general prayers that are said often and frequently. They are the most common prayers and are used daily. They are often recited the same way every time and are said frequently.*
- **Oriki Egun**: *These are prayers that honor and seek guidance, blessings, and wisdom from the ancestors.*
- **Oriki Iyere**: *Prayers asking for something, requesting something, or asking for help or support in life.*
- **Oriki Orin Iyin**: *These prayers are often sung to honor the divine and are part of a musical rhythm.*

In summary, prayer holds immense importance in the Yoruba spiritual tradition, fulfilling diverse roles for different purposes and events. Whether seeking guidance from the Orishas, paying respects to ancestors, or expressing gratitude to the divine, prayer acts as a crucial channel for communication and spiritual connection.

* * *

CHAPTER 7

SPIRITISM: WHAT IS IT?

AN INTRODUCTION TO SPIRITISM

SPIRITISM, also known as Espiritismo in Spanish or Kardecism, is a spiritualist philosophy founded by Allan Kardec in the mid-19th century in France. It spread throughout Europe and was incorporated into many indigenous and African-based religious traditions in Brazil, such as Umbanda and Candomblé. From Brazil, it spread to the Caribbean, becoming part of the Lucumi/Santería practices in that region.

Spiritism is based on the belief in the existence of spirits and their communication with the living. It teaches that the soul is immortal and, after death, enters a spiritual realm where it can continue to evolve and learn. This realm is believed to be divided into different levels, each corresponding to the spiritual development of the souls inhabiting it. Spiritists believe in reincarnation and that spirits can communicate with the living through mediums, who act as channels between the two worlds. Practices such as seances, meditation, and prayer are used to communicate with spirits. Spiritism emphasizes the importance of charity, kindness, and moral values in daily life.

The most basic belief of this philosophy is that the world is made up of two fundamental substances, matter and spirit. In the Yoruba diaspora, particularly in Candomblé, Umbanda, and Santería, Spiritism has been integrated into Orisha spirituality and ancestor veneration. Although Spiritism does not originate in Yoruba land, its teachings align with the Yoruba practice of ancestor veneration, and it is widely accepted across Yoruba diaspora communities. Spiritism holds that human beings are spirits inhabiting physical bodies and that communication with the spirit world is essential for receiving guidance. It also believes in the concept of karma, where every action has consequences, and that spiritual evolution is achieved through self-improvement and moral conduct.

WHAT IS UMBANDA?

Umbanda is a syncretic religion that grew out of a mix between the Yoruba Orisha tradition, Catholicism, Kardec Spiritism, and the indigenous beliefs of the Amazon natives. Umbanda evolved and originated in Brazil. Umbanda centers on the worship of the Orishás. The Orishas are seen as having the power or the Ase to assist and heal those in need and to provide guidance and protection to their followers. One unique key practice of Umbanda is the medium/priest. The Priests and Priestesses of this tradition are not only seen as mediums but must show some level of medium ability to be fully ordained within the religion. When the medium priest or priestess goes into a trance, he or she will often display physical signs of possession such as changes in his or her voice, behavior, and appearance. Umbanda also places a strong emphasis on charity and helping those in need. It is believed that by helping others, practitioners are also helping the Orishás and strengthening their own spiritual connection.

A Bóveda is a special altar or shrine used in Kardec Spiritism to honor various spirits. It is often a small table or cabinet in one's home or place of residence, sometimes located in a corner or in a part of the house that is secluded or private. The table often will have a white tablecloth spread over it and will often contain several glasses or goblets of water, each representing a particular spirit being honored, referred to as "las Fuentes," the spiritual sources. These cups are often filled with fresh water for the purposes of allowing the spirits to cleanse and purify the space, and the water should be clear and not murky. Other objects include, sometimes, a cross to symbolize the crossroads between the physical and spiritual world. A Christian cross or rosary may often be used, but it does not necessarily have the same meaning attached to it as it would in Christianity. The cross is a common symbol in Afro-Caribbean religions such as Santeria, Vodou, and Palo Mayombe, used to symbolize the gatekeeper as well as the different dimensions of the spirit and physical worlds, and at the center, they both come together. Other objects on the Bóveda may include various candles, flowers, and other offerings. The Bóveda is typically used as a focal point for prayer, meditation, and communication with the spiritual world. In Santeria, the Bóveda is used to honor a person's Egbe or heavenly mates, while an ancestor shrine would be used to honor your ancestors, which we talked about earlier, located on the floor in a corner of a room.

In Vodou, a Boveda is used to connect with the lwa, or spirits, and to ask for their help in various areas of life. In Palo Mayombe, the Bóveda is used to communicate with the spirits of the dead and to perform various magical rituals. A Boveda often has many glasses of fresh water, which are referred to as Fuentes. Each glass may represent a particular spirit or a particular spirit family. They are often organized on the mesa or table next to each other in various ways. The different ways they are organized may mean different things in different spiritual houses. When using glasses of water, either for a

Boveda or for an ancestor shrine, it is important to know how to read them.

How to Read the Fuentes (Glass of Water) on Your Bóveda or Ancestors' Shrine

It's important to understand what the spirits are communicating. When the water in a glass is murky or cloudy, it may indicate a need for further cleansing. This could mean you need to cleanse yourself, your ancestors' shrine, or your Boveda. It may also suggest you need to spend more time with your ancestors, your Egbe, or pay closer attention to their messages. Here's what you should do immediately:

1. Clean the glass and refill it with fresh, clean water.
2. Take note of the murky water.

It's often recommended to clean the room and the area around the altar, place fresh, colorful flowers nearby, offer the spirits something sweet, and take a bath. You can use the Obi Divination system to ask yes or no questions to understand the cause of the murky water or seek a divination reading from a trusted, reputable Priest or Priestess. If the water frequently becomes murky, it might be due to the water quality itself. However, if you rule this out, it's essential to find the spiritual cause.

Ask yourself: What in my life is unclear or murky? Am I under spiritual attack? Do I have significant emotional or physical stress? Am I attending to my mental and physical health and safety?

Once you think you've identified the issue, consult your ancestors. Use the Obi to confirm their responses. If they say yes, continue asking questions until you get clear answers. Begin by offering them basic items like water and light, and if needed, move to more specific offerings such as fruit or honey. If they confirm with a yes, then your consultation is complete. If they continue to say no, keep asking questions. Remember, they might be asking for something simple, like spending more time with them. If you become confused, it's best to consult a competent Priest or Priestess for guidance. Don't make assumptions.

READING BUBBLES IN WATER

If the water is clear but there are no bubbles in the glass, it normally indicates that further communication needs to be done, and a person needs to do divination and ask the ancestors what more they need. This is often an indication of the ancestors needing an offering. When we give our ancestors offerings, what we are doing is providing them with energy, and this energy is given to them so they, in turn, can transform it into the things we need in our lives. Not want but need. If there are bubbles, it normally indicates that the spirits are present, and everything is stable. It also indicates that the ancestors have received the offerings or our messages and are aware of what is going on. If the bubbles in the glass are not equally distributed, for instance, there are a lot of bubbles concentrated in one area of the glass and few in other areas of the glass, this can indicate that the relationship between the person and the ancestors is limited, and it needs to improve. This may mean the person needs to spend more time at their ancestors' shrine or Boveda. It may also mean that the spirits may be asking for something further.

Note: Bubbles often indicate that there is no heavy negative energy present around the individual. Bubbles can also indicate the process of clearing out negative energies as well. It is sometimes recommended that the person uses the water offered to the spirit in a bath or another way to help clean them if the person asks the spirit to do so.

* * *

Select a serene and calm location that is devoid of any disturbances or interruptions. Light a white candle and focus your attention on the flame.

Note: You should only use white candles on your ancestors' shrine or Boveda. Never use other colors, especially dark colors. The color white represents purity and high spiritual energy as well as peace and light.

Carefully watch the flame, taking note of its color, height, and movement. Pay close attention to any patterns exhibited by the flame, such as spirals, sparks, or abrupt changes in direction. Inquire with your spirit guides and ancestors for guidance and clarification on how to interpret the flame. Keep an open mind for any insights or messages that might come your way. Write them down so as not to forget them later when performing this task at a future time. Once finished, never blow out a candle but snuff it out instead.

Here are some basic interpretations of the candle flame. If the flame is tall and steady, it may be a sign of healthy positive energy in the atmosphere, and the spirits are at peace and are comfortable. If the flame is flickering or unsteady, it may be a sign that the flame is burning off some negative energy, or there may be a presence of some negativity. My recommendation is to burn some sage or lavender in the room. If you don't want to burn anything, you can use a spray bottle and spray fresh water with lavender oil or herb, or sage oil or herb mixed in it. Once you mix the herb or oil into the water within the container, drop a small quartz crystal or clear rock to the bottom of the container and shake it afterwards. You can use this water to spray in the corners of the room. It is recommended that you continue to let the fire burn (unless it is a hazard) until it either burns out or the flame becomes steady. If you need to extinguish it. You can ask your ancestors and spirit guides what is going on using obi divination. (Please see instructions on divination in the later chapters.) If the flame is flickering or unsteady, I recommend that you have not done so already, either change the water on the shrine that is closest to the candle, or put a glass of clear, cool water out on the shrine to balance the flickering flame and help clear the space. You may also want to use divination to ask the ancestors or spirit guides if they need any offerings at this time to help clear away any negativity and help strengthen them.

Note: a flame may be flickering or unsteady due to a draft in the area if the windows are open.

A bright, clear flame indicates clarity of purpose or intention, while a dim or smoky flame may indicate confusion or uncertainty. If the flame is dim or small, first look to see if water got into the candle or if there is a draft in the area. If not, follow my recommendations above if you get a flickering or unsteady flame. A dim flame may indicate that you need to clean your shrine. Again, when in doubt, ask them through divination! A spiral or other unusual pattern in the flame may represent a message or guidance from the spirit world. In this situation, you can use divination to find out what that message is. I also suggest you go get an Ifa reading by a competent Babalawo or Iyanifa. It's important to remember that reading a candle flame is not an exact science, and different people may interpret the flame differently. The most important aspect of this practice is to remain open and receptive to the guidance and messages that may come through. It is about developing that sense of spiritual intuition that you get from working more closely with your personal spirit guides, which takes time to develop.

* * *

The art of using playing cards for divination is, in today's world, a lost art. I thought I would include it within this chapter because of its historical importance amongst many of the old school traditionalists. This traditional form of divination is still practiced and can be found in Cuba amongst Santeria practitioners, where they use the Spanish playing card deck, and amongst spiritualists in Haiti. Like the minor arcana in the Tarot deck, each suit often symbolizes a particular theme or elemental energy that is believed to manifest in various ways within life.

When reading the cards, we often pick five cards from the deck, with each card representing the following:

Card 1: The Past

Represents past events or circumstances that have led to the present situation.

Card 2: The Present

Reflects the current situation, an ongoing event, or an obstacle being faced.

Card 3: The Future

Indicates a future event, potential outcome, or something yet to unfold.

Card 4: Guidance for the Present

Provides clarity, advice, or guidance regarding the second card. Place this card above the second card.

Card 5: Guidance for the Future

Offers clarity, advice, or guidance related to the third card. Place this card above the third card.

* * *

INTERPRETING THE CARDS

Suit of Spades

In divination, Spades are often associated with the element air and with the suite of Swords within both the Tarot and the Spanish card deck. When Spades appear in a reading, it is believed they represent challenges, obstacles, and conflicts, as well as issues that we may need to work on in our lives.

1. **Ace of Spades:** This card may indicate sudden changes, transitions, and is equivalent to the death card in the Tarot deck. Note: death is the end of one cycle or situation in our life, so another cycle can begin. Death often does not mean physical death. This card could indicate that something needs to change in our lives for the better when it appears. The death of a situation or circumstance in our life that is harmful to us may be a positive thing.
2. **Two of Spades:** This card may indicate some obstacles or challenges and sudden unexpected occurrences. It may indicate a difficulty with making decisions.
3. **Three of Spades:** This card may indicate Sorrow, sadness, loss, or grief. Grief and sadness may have taken hold in the past and still affect us currently; perhaps we may need to heal from this to move on to the next chapter in our lives. This card could also indicate an underlying past internal emotional state that still lingers within us, which could affect our future relationships or situations, and our state of mind.
4. **Four of Spades:** This card may indicate an illness or health issue, may also indicate the need for healing and recovery, as well as rest, retreat, and meditation. One should consider

concentrating more on one's own personal health and needs.

5. **Five of Spades:** This card may indicate conflict, challenge, competition, or change. This card may also point to a possible need for change or something we are dealing with that is difficult in some aspect of our lives. When this card appears, it may point to a much-needed change or relocation in our environment due to the inability to grow.

6. **Six of Spades:** This card may indicate stress, anxiety, as well as mental anguish or feeling burdened by someone or something in life. This card may also indicate a sense of loneliness as well as inner turmoil. When this card shows up, it may indicate that it is important at this time to address our mental well-being.

7. **Seven of Spades:** This card may indicate deception, trickery, secrecy, hidden information, and not being able to see the entire situation in a particular situation.

8. **Eight of Spades:** This card may indicate overcoming a difficult situation and the importance of trying to find healing from past events and or trauma.

9. **Nine of Spades:** This card may indicate witchcraft, accidents, and bad luck. The Nine of Spades tends to be a warning that we need to be more alert to our life accidents and the circumstances that are taking place around us. This is also the Karma card, indicating the importance of having good moral behavior.

10. **Ten of Spades**: This card may indicate hitting rock bottom, unpleasant news, anxiety, and issues surrounding justice and the legal system.

11. **Jack of Spades**: This card may indicate challenges, obstacles, competition, and rivals. Manipulation, enemies, unhealthy relationships, and immaturity.

12. **Queen of Spades:** This card may indicate the need to utilize the wisdom, experience, and knowledge learned through a

difficult past to move forward. This card points to not repeating the same mistake twice.

13. **King of Spades:** This card may indicate authority, leadership, control, potential for intellectual growth, and advancement.

* * *

In divination, diamonds are often associated with the element earth and with either Pentacles or Coins within both the Tarot deck and the Spanish card deck. Diamonds often represent one's material possessions, money, and things of a physical matter.

1. **Ace of Diamonds:** This card may indicate new beginnings, financial opportunities, and prosperity.
2. **Two of Diamonds:** This card may indicate partnerships, contracts, negotiations, agreements, and competition in the business world. This card is seen as two rivals competing.
3. **Three of Diamonds:** This card may indicate collaboration, teamwork, mastery, business relationships, and the building of financial wealth.
4. **Four of Diamonds:** This card may indicate hoarding, possessiveness, fear of loss, as well as possible troubles ahead with business or money.
5. **Five of Diamonds:** This card may indicate finding the solution to a difficult problem that may improve one's situation.
6. **Six of Diamonds:** This card may indicate instability, uncertainty, and hardships.
7. **Seven of Diamonds:** This card may indicate patience, perseverance, and the need to be content with what one has currently to move forward.

8. **Eight of Diamonds:** This card may indicate the need to stand back and think before one decides on something.

9. **Nine of Diamonds**: This card may indicate success, financial stability, business growth, Self-sufficiency, and independence.

10. **Ten of Diamonds:** This card may indicate wealth, legacy, or an unhealthy obsession with materialism or money that is clouding moral judgment.

11. **Jack of Diamonds:** This card may indicate practicality, resourcefulness, adaptability, and flexibility.

12. **Queen of Diamonds:** This card may indicate practicality, resourcefulness, practical intelligence, and common sense.

13. **King of Diamonds:** This card may indicate male energy, authority, and wealth. It may indicate the presence of a strong, authoritative male figure or the potential for financial success and stability.

* * *

SUIT OF CLUBS

In divination clubs or wands are often associated with the element fire within both the Tarot deck as well as the Spanish card deck, and often represent creativity and inspiration and your plans as well as opportunities in life.

1. **Ace of Clubs:** This card may indicate success, achievement, victory, creative energy, Inspiration, creativity, new beginnings.

2. **Two of Clubs:** This card may indicate decisions, choices, and opportunities in the future. This card often points to hopes and dreams to come.

3. **Three of Clubs:** This card may indicate growth, expansion, progress, and partnerships with others to make things

happen. The need to work well with others as a necessary element for achieving success in a project.

4. **Four of Clubs**: This card may indicate the need for hard work, productivity, growth, and determination to get through the obstacles to achieve one's goals.

5. **Five of Clubs**: This card may indicate conflict, competition, and challenges.

6. **Six of Clubs**: This card may indicate success, victory, progress, and growth.

7. **Seven of Clubs**: This card may indicate defensiveness, standing up for oneself, and perseverance.

8. **Eight of Clubs**: This card may indicate effort, hard work, progress, growth, Movement, and swift action.

9. **Nine of Clubs**: This card may indicate achievements, rewards, recognition, honors, Resilience, perseverance, and determination.

10. **Ten of Clubs**: This card may indicate completion, Burden, responsibility, hard work.

11. **Jack of Clubs**: This card may indicate creativity, innovation, risk-taking, and entrepreneurship.

12. **Queen of Clubs**: This card may indicate independence, leadership, authority, self-reliance, a successful businesswoman.

13. **King of Clubs**: This card may indicate a businessman, prosperity, creativity, and an innovator, a creator of opportunity.

In divination, hearts or cups are often associated with the element water within both the Tarot deck and the Spanish card deck, and often represent emotions and relationships with others around us.

1. **Ace of Hearts:** This card may indicate the beginning of a new friendship or a new relationship; it may also indicate the beginning of new relationships in a new job, new city, or new community.

2. **Two of Hearts:** This card may indicate harmony, balance, partnerships, connections with others, and points to children and family.

3. **Three of Hearts:** This card may indicate celebration, joy, happiness, friendship, or may indicate some unexpected good or bad information.

4. **Four of Hearts:** This card may indicate that the person may need to trust their gut and listen to their intuition concerning a situation or a specific individual.

5. **Five of Hearts:** This card may indicate joy, harmony, and balance within relationships.

6. **Six of Hearts:** This card may indicate nostalgia, memories, childhood, or sadness due to past relationships and the need to resolve this trauma and grief to move forward with future relationships.

7. **Seven of Hearts:** This card may indicate dreams coming true.

8. **Eight of Hearts:** This card may indicate letting go, moving on, and change. One's actions can have an influence on one's surroundings.

9. **Nine of Hearts:** This card may indicate the need to be more generous with others so that happiness and satisfaction will manifest in one's life.

10. **Ten of Hearts**: This card may indicate contentment, emotional fulfillment, and harmony.
11. **Jack of Hearts**: This card may indicate friendliness, Romance, charm, and creativity.
12. **Queen of Hearts:** This card may indicate the need for nurturing, caregiving, empathy, and compassion.
13. **King of Hearts**: This card may indicate having unrealistic and unattainable expectations of others in one's relationships.

How to Interpret YES or NO Answers Using Cards

To interpret YES or NO answers with cards, start by drawing 4 cards at random. The color of the cards will guide your interpretation: Black cards generally indicate "NO," while Red cards suggest "YES." Once the cards are drawn, use the following guidelines to understand their meaning based on the number of red and black cards:

- **0 Red, 4 Black**: This combination indicates a firm "NO." The answer is clear, and the situation is unlikely to change.
- **1 Red, 3 Black**: This often suggests a "NO," but with a slight possibility of a "YES." While the odds are against it, circumstances could shift.
- **2 Red, 2 Black**: This combination represents uncertainty. The outcome is unclear, and you may need to rephrase the question, gather more information, or ask again later.
- **3 Red, 1 Black**: This suggests a "YES," though there is still a small chance of a "NO." The situation is favorable, but not guaranteed.
- **4 Red, 0 Black**: This combination strongly indicates a "YES." The answer is clear, and the likelihood of a different outcome is very low.

The way you phrase your question can also influence the answer you receive. Questions that are too vague or broad may lead to uncertain outcomes, while specific and clear questions are more likely to yield accurate and reliable results. Be mindful of how you word your questions to ensure they are focused and clear, as this can help guide the cards to provide more meaningful answers.

* * *

WHAT IS FLORIDA WATER?

Florida Water is a fragrant, cologne-like water, similar to traditional European eau de cologne, first created in the 1800s. Beyond its pleasant scent, it is widely used in Afro-Caribbean, Latin American, and New Orleans Hoodoo traditions for cleansing, protection, and attracting positive energy, helping to remove negativity and enhance rituals. While store-bought Florida Water is convenient, it often contains synthetic ingredients.

SPIRIT WATER
A Natural Florida Water Alternative

Spirit Water is a natural, homemade blend and a better alternative to store-bought Florida Water. Made from herbs, essential oils, and other natural ingredients, it provides the same spiritual benefits, including cleansing, protection, and attracting positive energy, without any artificial additives. In my experience, Spirit Water is much more powerful and effective for spiritual work. This is my personal recipe, but you are welcome to adjust it by adding or removing herbs and ingredients to create a blend that best aligns with you and your spiritual practice.

- **1 cup of vodka, rum, or another clear alcohol and 1 cup of distilled water** – *Acts as a natural preservative and energetic cleanser.*
- **Alcohol alternative:** *Mix 5 tablespoons of white vinegar with 2 cups of distilled water to cleanse and purify energy. For added protection, spiritual cleansing, and to help preserve the mixture, you can optionally add 1 tablespoon of sea salt.*
- **1–2 orange peels** – *Attract joy, prosperity, and positive energy.*
- **½ lemon peel** – *Promotes cleansing, protection, and the removal of negativity.*
- **1–2 teaspoons dried lavender buds** *(or a few drops lavender essential oil) – Brings peace, calm, and spiritual purification.*
- **1–2 teaspoons dried rose petals** – *Encourages love, harmony, and emotional healing.*
- **2–3 cinnamon sticks** – *Attracts success, abundance, and protection.*
- **Several whole cloves** – *Strengthens protection and spiritual resilience.*
- **1–2 teaspoons dried mint leaves** *(or a few drops of mint essential oil) – Invites clarity, coolness, and revitalizing energy.*
- **1 bay leaf** – *Symbol of prosperity, success, and manifestation.*
- **1–2 teaspoons dried sage leaf** – *Clears negativity and purifies the energy field.*
- **1–2 teaspoons of vanilla extract** *per 2 cups of liquid (alcohol or water base)*
- ***Optional: ½ teaspoon dried bergamot peel*** *(or 3–5 drops bergamot essential oil) – Enhances uplifting energy, joy, and emotional balance.*

- **1. Combine all herbs, peels, and spices** *in a clean glass jar or bottle. Add the alcohol (or vinegar-water mixture) and stir gently. Avoid using any ingredients you know may cause an allergic reaction.*
- **2. If using the distilled water version:** *Gently boil the water with all herbs, peels, and spices for about 2 minutes to reduce impurities or bacteria. Remove from heat, allow the mixture to cool completely, then add any essential oils. This process helps preserve freshness and enhances the blend's energetic potency.*
- **3. Seal the jar tightly** *and store it in a cool, dark place. Let the mixture steep for 3–5 weeks, shaking gently once a week to blend the energies.*
- **4. After steeping, strain** *the liquid through a fine mesh strainer or cheesecloth to remove all solids.*
- **5. Pour** *the finished Spirit Water into a clean glass bottle or spray bottle for use.*
- **6. Warning:** *For spiritual use only. Do not ingest.*

* * *

In conclusion, Spiritism teaches that reality extends beyond what is visible or tangible, unfolding through an ongoing interaction between matter and spirit. Through communication, ritual, and moral reflection, we enter a relationship with guiding spirits who support our growth. When practiced with humility, discipline, and ethical clarity, Spiritism becomes less about prediction or control and more about responsibility for how we live, how we evolve, and how consciously we engage with the subtle forces shaping our lives.

* * *

CHAPTER 8
THE ORI CONSCIOUSNESS

DEFINING CONSCIOUSNESS IN YORUBA SPIRITUALITY

IN YORUBA SPIRITUALITY, the *Ori* is a metaphysical concept that refers to the head, considered the source of one's inner consciousness. The term "*Ori*" directly translates to "head" in the Yoruba language. Within Yoruba spirituality, Ori typically encompasses both the physical head (*Ori-Ode*) and the inner consciousness (*Ori-inu*). In this chapter, our focus will be on the *Ori-inu*, representing the inner consciousness. Consciousness, in this context, refers to being aware of oneself and the world, encompassing thoughts, sensations, emotions, and self-awareness. Yoruba philosophy breaks down inner consciousness into three main components: the lower consciousness, the subconscious, and the super consciousness. Let's clarify these:

- *Lower Consciousness: This is our waking state of awareness, where we experience our daily thoughts, emotions, and interactions with the world.*

- **Subconscious:** *The subconscious serves two primary functions. Firstly, it processes the experiences, thoughts, and emotions from our lower consciousness. Secondly, it acts as a link between the lower consciousness and the super consciousness, facilitating communication between the two.*
- **Super Consciousness:** *This is the realm of higher awareness, holding our destiny, knowledge, and wisdom. It's where we receive messages from our heavenly twin, guiding us on our spiritual journey.*

* * *

THE ROLE OF ORI IN OUR LIVES AND ITS INFLUENCE ON ORISHA BLESSINGS

Our **Ori-inu** serves as an innate guide within us, offering support and direction throughout our journey within this lifetime. The Ori-inu has control over our destiny. The Orishas may bestow guidance and blessings upon us, but it's our Ori-inu's decision to accept or reject these blessings. Our *Ori-inu* also helps us to communicate with the Orishas, Ancestors, and Egbe as well.

Because of these reasons, it's essential to honor and care for our Ori, including both our physical head (ori-ode) and our (Ori-inu), so we can attract all the good things in life and have a clear head to guide us. From the instant we're born to the moment we draw our final breath, our Ori remains a steadfast source of support and guidance, accompanying us unfailingly throughout our entire journey here in this world. This is why it is crucial to first honor our Ori before Orishas.

The Odu: **Ogunda Meji** reminds us that our Ori is always by our side. Many people starting out on the path of Orisha spirituality seek to know the name of their guardian Orisha immediately, without realizing that they need to first learn how to take proper care of their Ori.

Their guardian Orisha is unable to offer them any support without the permission of their Ori first and foremost. Honoring our Ori opens a path for us to receive all the blessings from every other Orisha.

THE PARTS OF ORI-INU

Ori-inu consists of two main components: the *Iwa-inu* and the *Ori-apere*. The iwa-inu represents our inner character, embodying moral consciousness and spiritual strength. The(*iwa-inu ori*) is also the part of the Ori-inu that holds the person's spiritual Ase within it. More specifically, here are the parts that the Iwa-inu aspect of the Ori-inu is made up of:

- **The Atari**: Located at the crown of the head, Atari serves as the interface between our Ori and the heavenly twin. It is often seen as the part of our soul attached to the Ori.
- **The Igoke**: Controlling our spiritual growth and wisdom, Igoke guides and maintains our spiritual development.
- **The Oluṣo**: Acting as our inner guide or judge, Oluṣo embodies moral consciousness and aids in correcting our character as we evolve spiritually.
- **The Ipako**: This part houses all our Ase. The Ipako represents the reservoir of spiritual power within our Ori and is part of the Iwa-inu.

* * *

Upon death, when the Emi (soul) separates from the body and ascends to heaven, both Igoke and Ipako accompany it. Understanding these components helps us comprehend the intricate workings of our Ori-inu and the profound role it has in helping to guide and support us in life. The Iwa-inu is also linked to the Ori-apere and the Iponri (spiritual twin in heaven) through the Emi (soul) as well.

85

Now that we have discussed the parts that make up the Iwa-inu, let's discuss the parts that make up the Ori-apere, or the part of the Ori-inu that holds a person's destiny. The parts that make up the Ori-apere include the **Ayanmo, Akunlegba, Akunleyan,** *and* **Eewo**.

AYANMO

Ayanmo aspect of the Ori- Apere is the aspect of a person's destiny that doesn't change. The word Ayanmo can translate as (things that are fixed). Some things that are considered fixed according to the Yoruba include the family you are born into and your gender. It is also said that certain things in life, such as achievements and prosperity, could also be fixed. If these things come to pass for the person easily. Ayanmo are the things that cannot be changed. These are the things that were predetermined in heaven prior to the person's birth.

AKUNLEGBA

Akunlegba is the aspect of a person's Ori-apere, or their destiny, which is the part of the Ori that holds the qualities given to the person in heaven for them to fulfill the destiny they chose for themselves. The natural qualities a person is born with, such as intelligence, a certain personality, athletic skill, etc. These are seen as "innate" qualities. On the other hand, often when the Ori is born, it will slightly alter the destiny it chose for itself in heaven.

When this happens, the person may need some new qualities that were not given to him in heaven. The person here on earth will learn and develop the new qualities needed to achieve this new and slightly changed destiny. These "learned" qualities don't, however, come as easily as the innate ones and may take many years of learning here on earth to acquire. The Akunlegba is also seen as part of the person's Ori-Apere that brings opportunities into the person's life. If the person has the qualities needed at the time these opportunities present themselves, then the person can achieve natural

86

success; if not, however, the person may fail to achieve a given thing in life. We often perform divination and sacrifice to One's Ori to help bring new opportunities to us. Sacrifice also serves to make it easier for us to develop our skills.

Sacrifice could, in part, unlock a person's Akunlegba, making it easier for them to learn a new skill to achieve a certain purpose as a part of their altered destiny. Akunlegba is considered much harder to change than the next aspect of a person's destiny that we will discuss, called the Akunleyan; however, a person's Akunlegba is still easier to change than the Ayanmo.

AKUNLEYAN

This aspect of a person's Ori-apere is often considered the choices we make as well as our conscious desires, dreams, and wishes that we hope to achieve. It is important to align the Akunleyan with both the Akunlegba and the Ayanmo. When all three are aligned together, it enables the person to have a successful life.

EEWO

Eewo is the part of the Ori that houses a person's taboos. Eewo, which translates as "that which is forbidden," these are the person's Spiritual taboos. Some of the Eewo are given in heaven during divination, others are given later when on earth. This aspect of the Ori tells us what things we should avoid in life to have a healthy, happy, long life. In conclusion, Ayanmo is "the things that are fixed and unchangeable," Akunleyan is our "purpose and desire," and Akunlegba is the power that we must manifest the opportunities in our lives and is the part of the Ori that holds those qualities, either learned or innate. The parts of the Ori, when in alignment with the person's true destiny, seems to work together harmoniously. Our Ori has the power to not only influence our lives but also manifest our deepest desires if all its parts are in direct alignment.

What is the Iponri?

The Iponri is another aspect of the person that influences the direction of their Ori; however, the Iponri is separate from the Ori and is the part of the person's soul that broke off and stayed in heaven. The Iponri allows us to have a spiritual connection to heaven and to the orisha. This connection comes through our Atari or our crown. This is where our Emi resides and is connected to the rest of our Ori-inu. Because the Iponri is an aspect of the Emi, they are the same thing and can communicate with each other through telepathy. The Iponri is often described as a mirror aspect of ourselves in heaven. The Iponri helps us communicate with our ancestors, the orisha who provide us with guidance here on earth. The Iponri also helps our Emi clearly understand our true purpose here on earth.

On the Topic of Emi

The Emi, more commonly called the soul, is composed of several parts. First, being the part of the Emi or soul that connects us to heaven and the spirits, which is our heavenly twin or our Iponri, and the second part is the part of our soul that connects us to God. Our Iponri allows us a connection with the spirit world, and our imọle ibukun, which is the breath of Olodumare, connects us to feel and experience God both in this world as well as in heaven. The imọle ibukun is the highest aspect of the emi. The Emi also holds both the Igoke and the Ipako aspects of the Ori once the earthly life is completed.

Determining Alignment and Destiny

Being in alignment with one's destiny is essentially the goal of the entire Yoruba spiritual practice. We go to divination to check if we are in alignment or out of alignment with our destiny. The concept of alignment with one's destiny is paramount in almost every part of

Yoruba spirituality. When we look at the divination process in IFA, we often see that a client will come for a consultation when their life is not going well.

The diviner then checks with IFA to determine if the client's life is either out of alignment or in alignment with their destiny. If a client is out of alignment with their destiny, things in their life often are not working out well for them. This is a good indicator that a person is out of alignment, but one cannot be certain until the consultation is done. During a consultation, you will often hear the terms "Ire" and "Ibi" or "Osogbo." "Ire" means being in alignment with one's destiny, while "Ibi" and "Osogbo" often refer to misfortune, indicating that someone is not aligned with their destiny. The word "Ibi" actually means "to question something"; often, this refers to questioning the misfortune in our lives. These terms are always used in divination consultations within the Orisha Tradition.

To explain further, a client can either be in Ire or in Ibi; there is no third option. If you do not hear these terms during a consultation, be cautious of the person performing it. More details are provided in chapter seventeen if you wish to skip ahead. If a person is determined to be in Ire, or blessings, it usually means they are aligned with their spiritual destiny. The Diviner or Babalawo will often suggest offering a sacrifice to an Orisha or one's Ori to either strengthen the existing Ire or change Ibi to Ire. If a client is determined to be in Ibi during the consultation, it likely means they are not aligned with their spiritual destiny. The Diviner will recommend a sacrifice, as indicated by Ifa, to change this misfortune into Ire or blessings. This act is believed to realign the person with their spiritual destiny.

There could be scenarios where a person can be in sync with their spiritual path despite facing misfortune. For instance, they might need to fulfill sacrifices that needed to be done in heaven prior to coming to Earth or sacrifices that were promised in heaven to be completed once they arrive on Earth to gain the blessings necessary for fulfilling their destiny. These sacrifices, known as Ebo, could be an integral part of their life journey. It's conceivable that they made a commitment in the spiritual realm to complete these sacrifices during their earthly existence. This is just one instance where someone could be both in Osogbo and in alignment with their destiny. Another scenario is that misfortune could enter one's life due to not fulfilling a commitment to Egbe or Ori. A third possibility is that misfortune arises due to violating their Eewos or taboos, which brings them out of alignment with their destiny. If misfortune results from the person's ignorance or violation of their taboos, it often indicates they are no longer in alignment.

In Yoruba spirituality, Iwa Pele is seen as a fundamental part of maintaining balance in the natural order. When we uphold the principles of Iwa Pele, our energy remains intact, forming a protective barrier around us. This barrier shields us from negative forces like Osogbo or misfortune. However, if we neglect these principles, our energy field weakens, creating openings through which harmful energies can penetrate, leading to chaos in our lives and health. Conversely, when we embody Iwa Pele, we accumulate more positive energy, fortifying our protective shield against misfortune. The energy we emit through our actions, thoughts, and words influences what we attract back into our lives. When aligned with Iwa Pele, this energy can bring healing and blessings. But if we stray from these principles, our energy field weakens, inviting further chaos. Essentially, our alignment with Iwa Pele determines whether we attract positivity or negativity into our lives.

HOW DOES THIS RELATE TO DESTINY?

It is believed that following the principles of Iwa Pele is a part of everyone's destiny. By doing this, it is believed that not only will the universe bring Ire "blessings" to you, but that Ire will naturally align you with your spiritual destiny by bringing opportunities into your life. It has been said that if a person does not know what their spiritual destiny is, they just need to practice good, gentle Iwa, character, and they will be naturally aligned with their spiritual destiny by the continuous practice of good Iwa. Past and future good moral behavior, or Iwa-Pele, may also sometimes be taken in place of a physical Ebo or offering by an Orisha and serve to help the person fulfill the various Ebos or sacrifices needed to clear their path for them to achieve their destiny.

THE JOURNEY FROM HEAVEN TO EARTH

In the beginning of time, Olodumare created from a piece of his own essence the Irunmole and all the spiritual beings in heaven. Olodumare's divine light expanded outwards, creating all spirits. After this, the heavens were created. Once these things had taken place, Olodumare and the spirits decided to create the world. At this time, the spirits in heaven would travel to earth and help build the earth so that one day the earth can be as beautiful as heaven. The journey to Earth serves a purpose to purify the soul through various trials.

*When Emi (soul) decides to go to the earth, the first thing it does is it goes to Ifa and tells Ifa what it desires to accomplish upon the earth. Ifa then provides an Odu for Emi with various Sacrifices, it must be completed either in heaven or as soon as it arrives upon the Earth. Following this, Emi presents the Odu to **Ajala-mopin,** who is the divine carver, and requests Ajala to carve for him a head based on the Odu received from Ifa, as well as a price Emi decides to pay for the Ori. The currency is believed to be some of Emi's own Ase that he has accumulated either in heaven or in prior lifetimes.*

Emi then tells Ajala the qualities that he desires to have upon the earth. Ajala then carves out these qualities as a part of the head Emil will wear once he arrives on earth. Ajala then gives Emi a choice of several heads, and Emi picks the Ori best suited for him and the tasks he wants to accomplish when on Earth. The amount of Ase Emi is willing to pay Ajala also determines the Ori Emi can receive as well. Once Emi acquires Ori at Ajala's house, a piece of the Emi is broken off, and this piece becomes the Iponri or the spiritual twin in heaven. The broken part of Emi attaches to the Ori, and this continues until the earthly existence is finished, and Emi can reattach itself to its twin upon its return to heaven. Following this painful separation, the Ori begins its long journey to the Earth.

As the Ori travels across the dark abyss onto the earth and into the womb, it becomes forgetful and loses much of its memory of the heavenly realms. It is also said in some lineages that the Iponri is, in fact, the part of the soul that houses the memories of the heavens, which must stay in heaven.

* * *

SECTION TWO
The Ori Alignment Ceremony

The Ori alignment ceremony is performed with the purpose of aligning all the components of the Ori-inu. This ceremony is believed to enable those who go through it to become more aware of their own potential and destiny. Alignment takes place when the individual's higher consciousness is shifted directly above their lower consciousness. This can happen naturally, but is facilitated by honoring one's own Ori. Honoring One's Ori can be done by prayer or through giving offerings to Ori, commonly called "feeding Ori" by the Yoruba traditionalists.

The lower consciousness sometimes produces a cloudy image in front of the person's spiritual eye that prohibits the person from seeing directly and clearly. Much of this can be cleared up by strengthening our Ori through either offerings or prayer, as well as fixing our moral character. This cloudiness is often caused by bad moral behavior or the trauma and emotional baggage we continue to carry and accumulate. If this cloudiness continues to accumulate, it is believed it can make us sick and soil our destiny. This dark energy damages our ability to live for today and is believed to prevent the person from seeing what is in front of them, pulling them backwards and out of alignment while they move forward. This cloudiness we believe not only prevents clarity but can often prevent the Ori-inu from opening to receive blessings.

We clear out this negative energy by first cleaning the Ori by a ceremony called an Ibori and then by feeding it with various offerings. We believe one can slowly start to realign the person to their true purpose in life. The Ibori ceremony may need to be repeated multiple times, however, to reach optimal results. This may include abstaining from various foods and other things afterwards as well.

The Ori ceremony has three major aspects to it. The first is a divination reading that is most often performed. After this, an Ibori is performed, followed by the receiving of the Ile Ori shrine icon. This icon is traditionally always made up of cowrie shells and is given to the person as a focal point for honoring their Ori-inu. This icon represents the person's Ori and is often given, especially in traditional IFA. Feeding and appeasing one's Ori is believed to enhance self-healing abilities, as well as heighten clairvoyant and intuitive capacities, among other benefits. A significant advantage of clear communication and alignment with one's Ori is the ability to manifest personal destiny. This heightened state of awareness enables individuals to materialize the desires of their Ori-inu in their everyday lives. This state of consciousness, often referred to as "enlightenment" in other various world traditions such as Buddhism and is simply achieved by aligning and facilitating communication between the two aspects of a person's consciousness.

One way to keep your Ori clear is to practice daily cleanliness in body, mind, spirit, and actions. The energies we create through our actions and our thoughts have a unique vibration that affects our physical body and health, as well as what things in our lives manifest around us. If we send out good vibes, it's believed that we will receive them back. On the other hand, if we send out negativity, we may receive that energy back. The Yoruba believe that like energies tend to attract like energies. An Ibori can serve to rid the Ori of all the bad accumulated energy around them; however, if the person continues to send out the same destructive thoughts and actions, they will not be clean for very long. If someone goes outside and rolls in the mud, then takes a bath, and afterwards once again rolls into the mud, how beneficial could the bath have been if the person were to just go out and come completely filthy again after a bath? Both cleanings and offerings are meant to strengthen and bring blessings.

OTHER FOOD ITEMS OFFERED TO ORI

- **Cool water:** Symbolizing purity, cleansing, and rejuvenation, it serves as a fundamental ingredient in most ceremonies, bringing a coolness to the situation.
- ***What is an Omiero?*** An Omiero is a mixture of herbs and water that commonly incorporates herbs into the water.

One example of this would be to boil the herbs in the water, then cool it down before its use.

- **Mint and Peppermint** help to cool down and calm down heated situations.
- **Sage**, belonging to the mint family, is used for purification and can also provide a cooling effect.
- **Basil** aids communication between consciousness levels, enhances clairvoyant awareness, and improves spirit communication in dreams. There are many other herbs you can use as well.
- **Fresh rose petals**: Symbolizing beauty, love, and divine blessings.
- **Honey**: Representing sweetness, abundance, and blessings.
- **Eggshells**: Associated with purification and growth.
- **Obi** (kola nut): Used as a divination tool to gain insights and guidance from Ori.
- **Bitter Kola**: to improve the person's health and to bring positive energy into life.
- **Coconut**: Symbolizing spiritual purity and the ability to overcome obstacles.
- **Fruits**: Representing abundance, vitality, and nourishment, they are occasionally offered to bring sweetness into life.
- **Lavender:** This herb can be offered to ward off negative energy and negative thoughts.
- **Gin /Rum**: Offered for strength and perseverance.
- **Palm oil**: Used for protection against illness, purity, and protection.

It is customary to consult Obi Divination before offering any item to Ori, ensuring that the offerings will yield positive results.

In conclusion, honoring One's Ori through either ceremonies or personal devotion serves to help align you and help you tap into your full potential as well as understand your destiny. When we engage in these practices and rituals, we can establish a relationship with our Ori. By cleansing the Ori through the Ibori ceremony and providing offerings, individuals can gradually realign themselves with their true-life purpose.

* * *

CHAPTER 9

THE YORUBA CALENDAR

THE YORUBA PEOPLE have a fascinating traditional calendar called the "*Kójódá*," which means "may the day be clearly foreseen." This unique calendar blends the cycles of the sun and the moon, making it a lunisolar calendar. Today, it's often observed using a mix of the 7-day week from the Gregorian calendar and the traditional Yoruba lunar calendar. The Gregorian calendar, based on the sun, was believed to be introduced during the colonization period. In the Yoruba calendar, a week is only four days long. This comes from the belief that the world originally had four corners at its creation. So, while we're used to a week being seven days, in the Yoruba calendar, it's just four. Each month has seven of these 4-day weeks, making a month 28 days long. Unlike the Gregorian calendar's 12-month cycle, some scholars think the ancient Yoruba had a 13-month cycle, giving them 364 days in a year with an extra day that might have taken place during the New Year Celebration in July/August or during the IFA Festival in June. Some Scholars also believe that the 13-month ancient lunar calendar cycle might have started on either the New moon or the full moon. In the Yoruba calendar each of the four days of the Yoruba week is dedicated to a specific Orisha. People honor

these Orishas on their respective days with various rituals and celebrations. Here is an overview of which Orishas correspond to each of
the four days in the traditional calendar:

DAY OF OBATALA (OJO OBATALA)
This is the first day of the week and is dedicated to honoring the
Orishas Obatala, Egungun, Iyaami, and Babalu-Aye. The first day
was given to Obatala because he was the oldest

DAY OF ORUNMILA (OJO ORUNMILA)
This is the second day of the week and is dedicated to honoring the
Orishas Orunmila, Esu, Oshun, Yemoja, Aje, IFA and Olokun, Egbe.

DAY OF OGUN (OJO OGUN)
This is the third day of the week and is dedicated to honoring the
Orishas Ogun, Oshosi, and Oko.

DAY OF SANGO (OJO SANGO)
This is the fourth day of the week and is dedicated to honoring the
Orishas Shango and Oya.

* * *

If you choose to follow the traditional days of the Yoruba week and
want to calculate the specific days, I recommend using a digital
calendar on your phone, laptop, or any device with a built-in
calendar program that has a "repeat event" function. You may need
to go online or consult an elder to determine the specific Gregorian
calendar dates for each day. Once you have the starting dates, follow
these steps: Open your digital calendar, go back to the starting dates,
and set the events to repeat every four days indefinitely:

1. **06 // 15 // 2024 - Ojo Obatala**
2. **06 // 16 // 2024 - Ojo Orunmila**

3. **06 // 17 // 2024 - Ojo Ogun**
4. **06 // 18 // 2024 - Ojo Sango**

After **Ojo Sango,** the cycle of days continues in the same order: **Ojo Obatala (06 // 19 // 2024), Ojo Orunmila (06 // 20 // 2024), Ojo Ogun,** and so on, repeating continuously. By setting this four-day cycle in your calendar, you can calculate all future occurrences of these days, making it easy to track them over time.

THE FOURFOLD RHYTHM OF THE SELF

The traditional four-day week *Obatalá, Orunmila, Ogun, and Ṣàngó* forms a sacred rhythm of inner development: peace, insight, action, and balance. Each day builds upon the last, moving from stillness to understanding, from effort to harmony. Living in alignment with this rhythm encourages mindful self-mastery, reminding us that peace is the foundation of wisdom, wisdom guides action, and action must ultimately return to balance. To live by this calendar is to recognize that each day is a step in the unfolding of one's destiny, guided by divine energies that shape both the cosmos and the human soul.

WHAT IS ITADOGUN?

Itadogun is a sacred period that occurs every 16 days, with the observance on the 17th day in the traditional Yoruba calendar. During this time, followers and devotees of Orunmila and Ifá seek guidance and blessings through divination and perform various rituals to align with their destiny and gain insights into their personal lives. Many Orisha practitioners visit the Temple or consult their Babalawo for guidance from Ifá on this day. Different communities have different schedules for observing Itadogun. Some observe it once a month, while others, as mentioned, observe it every 16 to 17 days. Personally, I observe Itadogun on the full moon of every month, as it is the only time I can set aside from my busy life. The key is to observe Itadogun regularly, regardless of the exact frequency, as maintaining the practice is more important than the specific timing.

THE SEVEN - DAY WEEK CYCLE FOR OBSERVANCE

Observing the orishas according to the 7-day week cycle is increasingly common outside of Africa today. Those who choose this approach find it simpler to connect specific Orishas with particular days of the week. Here are the days of the week and their associated Orishas under this system, although it differs from the traditional 4-day week observed in some practices.

OJO-AIKU / SUNDAY
Sunday is considered a day for blessing long life and settling disputes. It's a good day to ask for peace, protection, and good health. The Orishas honored on this day include Obatala, Ori, Olodumare, Orunmila, and IFA.

OJO-AJE / MONDAY
Monday is known as the "day of money," marking the day the Orisha Aje came down to earth. It's a good day to ask for prosperity and financial blessings. The Orishas honored on this day include Eleggua/Eshu and Orisha Aje.

OJO-ISEGUN / TUESDAY
Tuesday is traditionally considered the day of victory. It's a good day to ask for help in overcoming obstacles and triumphing over enemies. The Orishas honored on this day are Ogun and Oshosi.

OJO-IRU / WEDNESDAY
Wednesday is a good day to honor your ancestors and give thanks for the blessings in your life. It is believed that ancestors visit most frequently on this day. However, it's not an ideal day to start new

projects. The Orishas honored on this day are Oya, Egungun, Babalu-Aye, and Egbe. It's also a good day to honor Mother Earth.

Ojo-Bo / Thursday

Thursday is a great day to start a new project or lay the foundation for an idea or task you've been putting off. It's also a perfect day for spontaneity and celebrating, especially with friends or family. The Orishas honored on Thursday include Shango and Ori.

Ojo-Eti / Friday

Friday is a good day for moving or clearing out old clutter. It's also ideal for removing negative obstacles that hinder progress, performing spiritual cleanings, and taking spiritual baths. It's a great day to finish up projects and complete tasks that have been left unfinished. The Orishas honored on this day are Oshun, Eshu/Elegua, Ori, Egungun, as well as any other Orishas you choose to honor beyond those honored on previous days.

Ojo-Abameta /Saturday

On this day we also finish up projects that we may not have completed during the prior days just as on Ojo- Ete. This is also a day we honor our mothers. Orishas honored on this day are: Yemoja, Olokun,Osain, Egungun and Ori as well as any other orishas you may decide to honor.

* * *

THE MOON PHASES AND THEIR MEANINGS

New Moon

New beginnings and a new start: darkness of the moon is symbolic to the darkness of the womb before birth. This is a time to plant new projects. This can be a time to honor Egbe and Egungun. The new moon symbolizes new beginnings, growth, and spiritual renewal. It is a time to set intentions, make plans, and start new projects.

Full Moon

A period of full clarity when things come into focus. The moon is illuminated completely by the light of the sun. This is a good time to work with your Ori. This is a time when confusion is illuminated by the light and things are seen for what they really are. A good time to seek insight into a problem that may be puzzling. The full moon symbolizes illumination, enlightenment, and spiritual power. It is a time for heightened intuition, divination, and manifestation.

Waning Moon

This is a good time to do magical tasks related to winding down and bringing things to an end. A good time to do cleanings, to expel bad energy and removal of negative energy as well as anything related to protection and healing. This is a time for rest and rejuvenation. The waning moon symbolizes release, letting go, and shedding old habits or patterns. It is a time to reflect on what is no longer serving you and release it to make space for new growth.

Waxing Moon

This is a time to do magical tasks related to growth. As the moon is moving out of the darkness and into the light. The waxing moon symbolizes growth, abundance, and manifestation. It is a time to focus on positive energy and work towards achieving your goals.

Dark Moon

The dark moon symbolizes rest, introspection, and spiritual transformation. It is a time to connect with your inner self, release negative energy, and prepare for new beginnings.

* * *

YORUBA FESTIVALS AND CELEBRATIONS

THE IFA FESTIVAL

The Ifa Festival often takes place in May or June, and some communities mark the New Year around this time as well. Celebrations honor the Orisha Orunmila and Ifa through a series of rituals, ceremonies, and gatherings. In Oyo, Nigeria, the festival involves key activities such as processions, purification and renewal rituals, and divination sessions. This time signifies renewal and fresh beginnings, celebrated with rituals and gatherings that honor the cycle of life and nature.

OLOJO FESTIVAL

The Olojo festival is an annual festival celebrated in Ile-Ife, Osun State, Nigeria, to commemorate the creation of the universe and the first dawn. The festival typically takes place in September or October and is characterized by the appearance of the Ooni of Ife, who is regarded as the custodian of Yoruba culture and tradition. During the festival, the Ooni is believed to visit the sacred grove to receive blessings and renew his spiritual connection with his ancestors.

OSUN-OSOGBO FESTIVAL

The Osun-Osogbo festival is an annual festival celebrated in Osogbo, Osun State, Nigeria, to honor the river goddess, Osun. The festival is typically held in August and is marked by several activities, including a procession to the Osun River, a prayer session, and a traditional dance known as the Bata dance.

EGUNGUN FESTIVAL

The Egungun festival is an annual festival celebrated by the Yoruba people to honor their ancestors. The festival is typically held in August or September and involves the wearing of elaborate costumes and masks by participants to represent the spirits of the ancestors.

The festival also features traditional music, dance, and rituals that are believed to honor and appease the ancestors.

EYO FESTIVAL

The Eyo festival is a popular festival celebrated in Lagos, Nigeria, to commemorate the death of a prominent Lagosian. The festival is typically held in February or March and is characterized by a procession of masquerades known as the "Eyo" or "Adamu Orisha Play." The festival is also marked by traditional music, dance, and other cultural activities.

SANGO FESTIVAL

The Sango festival is an annual festival celebrated in honor of Sango, the Yoruba god of thunder and lightning. The festival is typically held in August and is marked by several activities, including a procession to Sango's shrine, the wearing of red and white attire, and traditional drumming and dancing.

THE OSHUN OSOGBO FESTIVAL

A festival that is celebrated annually at Oshun-Osogbo grove in Nigeria as well as in the diaspora. The annual Oshun Festival takes place in August and lasts at least 5 days. The festival celebrates the Orisha Oshun. The legend behind the festival is that Oshun appeared to a group of travelers when they were at the riverbank of the Oshun River located near Oshun-Osogbo grove and told them that whoever offers her sacrifice at this time will receive the blessings of prosperity, wealth, abundance, and protection from her. It is said this festival and legend is over five hundred years old. Outside Yorubaland, this is a time to honor Oshun and offer her something at the riverbank in keeping with the legend.

THE ORO FESTIVAL

The Oro festival is a traditional festival celebrated by the Yoruba people, primarily in southwestern Nigeria. It is a secret society festival that is only attended by initiated men who are members of the Oro society. Women and uninitiated men are not allowed to witness the festival or even speak of it. The Oro festival is usually held in honor of a deceased Yoruba monarch or notable figure. The festival involves the use of masks and costumes that are believed to represent the spirits of the deceased. The masks and costumes are made of wood or cloth and are adorned with colorful decorations. During the festival, the Oro society members usually gather in the early hours of the morning and parade through the town or village.

The society members are usually dressed in black robes and carry canes or staffs. They chant and sing songs in honor of the deceased, and the procession is accompanied by the sound of drums and other traditional instruments. As the procession moves through the town or village, the Oro society members visit different households and perform rituals to bless the homes and ward off evil spirits. The Oro festival is a significant event in Yoruba culture and is believed to be a time of spiritual renewal and cleansing.

EGUNGUN MASQUERADE FESTIVAL
Occurs in June around the new year. This festival is a communal honoring of the ancestors. Dancing fills, the streets and Egungun appears behind bands of colorful cloth and masks. In the diaspora June and July are months we pay close attention to our ancestors. It is said they visit us during this time of the year. This festival takes place in both Nigeria and Brazil.

FESTIVAL OF YEMANJA
Primarily observed in Brazil on January 1st, the Festival of Yemanja honors Yemoja, the Yoruba goddess of the ocean and motherhood. Devotees offer miniature boats laden with gifts and flowers to the sea, seeking Yemoja's blessings for fertility, protection, and prosperity in the coming year. The festival underscores the deep

cultural and spiritual connections between Yoruba traditions and
Afro-Brazilian heritage

* * *

In conclusion, most celebrations take place in the ile (ee-lay) or
house of a Priest or Priestess or leader where a Bembé is held in
the Diaspora. While in Africa this can be true for some lineages
many celebrations either take place in a Temple or out in the
open on the streets. During the festival the sacred Batá drums
are beaten, and the space is filled with dancing and music. Many
times, an orisha will possess a devotee or priest while in a
trance. Each Orisha has their own unique dancing style during
the possession. The process of being possessed is referred to as
being mounted and is like possession in other African traditions.

* * *

CHAPTER 10
DREAMS AND SPIRIT GUIDES

DREAMS HAVE LONG CAPTIVATED humans across various cultures, offering glimpses into the realms beyond our waking consciousness. In the Yoruba tradition, dreams are classified into two categories: prophetic and ordinary. Prophetic dreams are regarded as messages from spirits, providing guidance or forewarnings to the dreamer. On the other hand, ordinary dreams reflect the individual's daily experiences, thoughts, emotions, and feelings. Differentiating between these dream types can be challenging for some people, as an ordinary dream may contain a prophetic message, and a prophetic dream may appear as mundane events.

Within the Yoruba tradition, it is common to also go for a divination reading after having a dream, especially if someone is unsure of the meaning of the dream they had and is not sure if it's a message from the spirit world. We believe divination serves as a definitive, reliable method for discerning the true nature of the dream and its intended message. The Yoruba believe both mediumship and divination are gifts Olodumare and Orunmila gave to humanity to communicate with heaven while here on earth.

Understanding the Role of the Iponri (Spiritual Twin)

Every individual possesses a spiritual twin, known as the Iponri, in heaven. This twin is intimately linked to us and serves as a conduit for communication between our earthly selves and the spirit realm. The Iponri is formed from a fragment of our own soul or Emi and enables us to receive messages from the spirit world, including our ancestors and Egbe-Orun. It acts as a bridge, relaying conversations and insights from other spirits in heaven to our higher consciousness. This is, in fact, how mediumship and spirit communication work; it is our twin that communicates with our ancestors, our egbe-orun and the orishas. Our twin then delivers the message from heaven to us. This aspect of us stays in heaven when we come to earth. It is basically a piece of us that stays. The Yoruba believe that heaven is the place we resided before coming into the world, and it is the place we will again reside once we leave the world.

Understanding the Egbe Orun

It is believed that when we come to the earth from Orun/ heaven, we leave our friends behind. These spirits, unlike our ancestors, are not related to us. We, however, have a very strong connection to them. They are our dear friends and companions as well as the communities we belong to in heaven. They are the ones we left behind in heaven before we came here to earth. They are the ones we call Egbe. Our Egbe still tries to communicate with us here on earth, just as our ancestors in heaven also try to communicate with us through our iponri here on earth. Again, our dreams are often associated with both our Egbe and our ancestors, as well as our own Ori or head, telling us something more than they are with the Orishas. The Word "egbe" often translates to mean "society or association."

. . .

Humans possess both lower and higher consciousness. The lower consciousness houses our emotions, thoughts, and trauma, while the higher consciousness transcends these fleeting sensations and provides stability. Our higher consciousness is closely connected to our iponri and to our Ori-inu, which receives messages from our Egbe-Orun and ancestors, guiding and warning us. Sometimes when we dream, we can be tapped into this higher consciousness, while other times we are only tapped into our lower consciousness. Individuals gifted in mediumship and prophecy are able to tap into their higher awareness much faster than those who do not have this ability. For an untrained medium or for someone who does not have this ability, it can often become very difficult for them to distinguish between their ordinary dreams and prophetic ones. The solution is simple: using divination will often provide them with the same or even better results.

Divination is a valuable tool for distinguishing between these two realities and pinpointing what messages are being sent from Orun to us and what messages are ordinary feelings and assumptions. The divination process has both an objective and a subjective part to it. We will start by defining the subjective component of it. The subjective part of the divination process is when we hold the divination tools in our own hands and drop them onto the mat. It is at this point that all doubt is erased and destiny determines how they will land. The objective aspect is the change that occurs once the divination chain leaves our hands and hits the ground. Once it is dropped, the subjectivity is clarified into objective truth.

DO SOME OF OUR EGBE AND ANCESTORS LIVE HERE ON EARTH WITH US?

The short answer to this question is yes, they do. Our ancestors know this to be true. We have parents who are a part of our ancestral kindred here on earth. The people we call our parents in this lifetime may have been our great-great-grandparents in a past lifetime, or we may have been their parents in a prior lifetime. This kindred relationship remains throughout lifetimes both here and in heaven, as we go back and forth regardless of what role you or one of your ancestors takes in each lifetime you and they are alive.

WHAT ABOUT OUR EGBE?

Our Egbe, just like our ancestors, do not just exist in heaven but also exist here in the world. Due to Atunwa or rebirth, it is known that we all travel back and forth from Orun to the earth and from the world to Orun at various times. If you happen to be born at a certain time here on earth and one of your Egbe is also born at the same time, or you both make it your destiny to cross paths while both of you are here on earth, this will take place. Sometimes, Egbe are spouses or extremely close friends we meet here on earth and have an extremely strong bond with.

WHAT HAPPENS TO OUR HEAVENLY TWIN ONCE WE DIE
HERE ON EARTH AND RETURN TO HEAVEN?

Once we pass away, many Orisha Practitioners believe that our soul will once again reunite with our heavenly twin, our iponri, and once again we will become one single unified soul called Emi. It is also believed that the part of the soul that lived on earth will bring wisdom and knowledge and Ase to share with the iponri that was acquired during its life. This new knowledge and increase in Ase (divine power) will spiritually elevate the soul to a higher level once both parts of it are unified.

Many Orisha practitioners know of some of the various Egbe-Orun communities that exist in heaven. Many Babalawos can often tell someone which Egbe communities they are a part of in heaven. We, however, do not have knowledge of every single Egbe community in heaven, so we can only ask IFA if a person is a member of one of the communities we are aware of and have knowledge about. So, if someone happens to be from one of the Egbe communities that we don't know about, they will often be identified in the "other" or unknown community category. Below is a description of some of the Egbe communities we do know exist in heaven.

OVERVIEW OF DIFFERENT EGBE COMMUNITIES

Egbe Iyalode: This Egbe group is characterized by their maternal love and protective guardianship. They are known for their strong ability to alleviate physical and emotional suffering. Gifted with this ability as part of their earthly destiny, they serve as beacons of comfort and solace for those they support. They tend to help those who are associated with them heal and heal others.

Egbe Jagun: This Egbe community is characterized by its ability to defend and protect others. They are often seen as being strong warriors and possess the ability to help those they protect win fights, wars, and disputes.

Egbe Imo: Highly knowledgeable and intellectual. They possess an innate ability to grasp complex concepts swiftly and accurately, engaging in deep contemplation and discussion. They are revered as guardians and custodians of celestial knowledge in the heavens. They tend to help those they protect solve problems.

Egbe Aseyori: Esteemed for their artistic creativity and innovative spirit, this Egbe community excels as artists and visionaries, inspiring awe with their creations. They tend to help those they protect have peace and inspiration.

Egbe Alakoso: Renowned for their mastery of natural energy and divination, this Egbe community possesses a unique ability to sense and manipulate energy fields. They excel in reading and balancing energy. They tend to help those they protect expel negative energy and attract positive things in life.

Egbe Ayeraye: Endowed with the innate ability to accompany souls to earth, this Egbe group serves as divine companions.

Egbe Ikole Orun: As the architects of heaven, this Egbe community is responsible for its construction and maintenance.

Egbe Baale: This Egbe group is associated with rulers and Kingship. They tend to help those who are associated with them gain positions of leadership.

Egbe Iyalaje: This Egbe group is associated with business and the marketplace. They tend to help those who are associated with them gain wealth and money.

* * *

In conclusion, the Egbe-Orun consists of many groups fulfilling unique roles and working together with other divinities to ensure things work properly. It is possible for a person to be a member of more than one Egbe group. Also, there are likely thousands of Egbe communities in heaven; however, the ones mentioned above are the most well-known.

* * *

CHAPTER II
THE YORUBA LIFE CYCLE

AT THE BEGINNING OF LIFE, after a baby is born in traditional Yoruba land, a ceremony referred to as the Ikosedaye, also known as the Esentaye, is normally held. Esentaye means "Feet touch the ground." This ceremony is only performed for newborns within the first 16 weeks and never before the 3rd day of birth. A Babalawo will come to the house and do a divination reading for the baby. This ceremony may be done by Orisha Priests in some lineages. This ceremony may also vary throughout the regions; however, there are some common themes. First, either Ifa or Orisha is consulted to determine the child's birth sign and destiny (ìpín).

If a Babalawo is performing this divination, various questions will be asked during the consultation, including: did the child come with Orisha? If the answer is "yes," the child may need to be initiated into that orisha eventually. What is the birth sign? This reveals a pattern called an Odu, which may come with various taboos or prohibitions that the child should follow as he ages to prevent vulnerability in life. Another question that is asked is which ancestor was the child reborn as. There is a belief that our ancestors live again in the new generations. Determining who the child was in a prior life will help with determining a name for the baby. The naming ceremony is done after the Esentaye as a separate ceremony. The birth Odu is sometimes written upon a piece of wood and kept by the parents with an Ori icon that is sometimes given as well. The Esentaye ceremony can only be done within the first 16-week period. After 16 weeks, everyone, no matter what age, is initiated through the Isefa ceremony. During the consultation, if a Babalawo or Iyanifa is performing this ceremony, it is customary for the baby's feet to touch the Iyerosun powder on the Opon IFA (IFA board) and the Ikins (palm nuts) used for divination, as well as various types of herbs. Prayers are often recited, and it is important to complete the Ebos (Sacrifices) prescribed in the divination as soon as possible after the ceremony to ensure all negativity is removed from the newborn's path.

Note: All precautions in these ceremonies must always be taken to never put any child in harm's way or danger. We never feed a child any honey because it can be dangerous to the little one. It is important to always consult a knowledgeable Priest, and one should never attempt to perform any of these ceremonies without being first initiated and under the guidance of an experienced elder who has been properly trained to perform these ceremonies.

THE NAMING CEREMONY (LORUKỌ ỌMỌ)

After the Esentaye ceremony, normally between the 7th and 9th day of a baby's life, the naming ceremony takes place. Often, the ceremony takes place in the morning or before noon. The parents and the Babalawo come together to determine a name for the child. The Yoruba people take giving names to their children very seriously. There is a belief that the proper name can protect the child from harm throughout the child's life. The Yoruba also believe that giving the wrong name to a child can cause harm. Following the child receiving a new name, often the community and family will gather to see the baby and provide donations and gifts to the new parents throughout the day. Sometimes this gathering will take place on the following day to celebrate both the child's birth and the new parents. Afterwards, the Babalawo will often instruct the new parents to clean their home.

M<small>ARRIAGE</small>

Igbeyawo Ceremony, Traditional Yoruba marriage is a sacred and significant union between two families, not just two individuals. It is viewed as a social and religious institution, and the wedding ceremony is a celebration that involves many rituals and customs. The first step in the traditional Yoruba marriage process is the introduction ceremony, also known as ***"mo mi mo e."*** This is where the families of the bride and groom meet to discuss the union and get to know each other. The groom's family is expected to bring gifts such as kola nuts, wine, and other items to signify their intentions to the bride's family. If both families agree to the union, the next step is the engagement ceremony.

The engagement ceremony is known as "*Igba-nkwu*" or "*Igbeyawo.*" During this ceremony, the groom's family will bring more gifts to the bride's family, and the bride will receive an engagement ring from the groom. This is also the time when the couple and their families will discuss the dowry, which is usually paid by the groom's family to the bride's family. The traditional Yoruba wedding ceremony, also known as "*Igbeyawo,*" is a colorful and joyous occasion that involves several rituals and customs. It typically takes place in the bride's family home or a chosen venue. The bride and groom will wear traditional Yoruba attire, and their families and guests will also dress in traditional attire. During the ceremony, the bride's family will serve the groom and his family kola nuts and wine to signify their acceptance of the union.

The couple will then exchange vows and rings, and the groom will present the bride with a gift. Afterward, the couple will go through a series of rituals, such as tying the knot, jumping over a broom, and exchanging gifts, to signify their commitment to each other. After the wedding ceremony, the couple will go through a traditional Yoruba naming ceremony, where they will be given their traditional Yoruba names. The couple will also receive blessings from their families and elders, and a feast will be held to celebrate the union. Prior to marriage or the start of a new relationship, it is often recommended to seek out Ifa's guidance.

This is to ensure that the relationship is aligned with the destiny of both individuals. Even if you don't have a spouse or partner yet and are desiring to meet someone and eventually get married, it's also recommended to seek Ifa's guidance. By seeking consultation and performing the proper sacrifices (Ebos), we believe it improves the chances of finding a compatible spouse.

According to Ifa, human beings are encouraged to seek out a spouse for companionship, support, physical love, and to start a family. In Ifa, family is highly valued as it's considered the greatest bringer of blessings and Ase, and the ancestors depend on it. By establishing a family, we further the bloodline so that the ancestors can be reborn in future generations, and we become ancestors once we pass away. There are numerous Patakis (stories) within the Odu IFA that talk about the importance of a spouse. Within the Odu Ogbe-Sa, it talks about completing things and the blessings that come from having a spouse. Two halves make a complete whole. This Odu also talks about having multiple possible future contenders for marriage and not knowing which one will work out, and that one must seek the guidance of Ifa and perform sacrifices to find out. Another thing this Odu talks about is the work required to make things work, which includes relationships.

The Yoruba have a strong belief that death is not the end, and that the person continues as an ancestor or is reborn, as we have discussed in previous chapters. The word *Itutu* can often be translated as to elevate and cool down the spirit of the deceased person so they can move forward into the afterlife and not be continually attached to the things of the world. The *Itutu* ceremony serves several of the following purposes; to release or transfer religious items owned by the deceased persons including items that are believed to contain energies of the Orishas, to offer sacrifices to insure that the soul of the person has the strength to make the journey back to heaven and lastly the ceremony serves the purpose to help detach the souls of the person from the physical world so that it has no desire to stay around and instead moves forwards. The *itutu*brings closure to both the departed soul as well as to the departed person's family and friends.

The various items which contain the energies of the Orishas are often either given to a family member in the religion, a godchild of the deceased, or taken to a natural place in nature, such as a river, mountain, or a tree, and are left at these locations depending on what the Orishas have determined they want when asked. As soon as the Babalawo arrives, the Orishas, and sacred items are all placed on the floor near the body of the deceased, and one by one they are consulted and are asked through divination as to where they want to go. Following this, the babalawo or Iyanifa determines if the cause of death was from a natural cause or from some type of Spiritual harm or Witchcraft. If it is deemed to be the cause of some unnatural form of death or Witchcraft, the Babalawo will inquire if the soul of the deceased person is in danger on the other side from some malevolent spiritual entity and if the family of the deceased is in danger of harm as well. If it is deemed that either the soul of the deceased or their family is in danger from spiritual harm or Witchcraft, the Babalawo will, through IFA divination, prescribe a sacrifice to protect the soul of the deceased so that they can cross over and to protect the family as well. The Babalawo then begins the various sacrifices prescribed by Ifa, and the Orishas are given away or brought to the river.

Note: *A sacrifice is always given to Eshu to open the doors, help guide, and protect the soul on its journey, even if it does not come up in the consultation.*

THE 2ND DAY

The Babalawo begins this process by purifying the body through prayers, smoke, and herbs. The Babalawo at this time invokes the soul of the deceased, explaining to them that they are dead and that after the final rites, they must begin their long journey to Orun. The Babalawo then asks the Orishas, ancestors, and God to protect the soul of the deceased from any evil upon their journey. The preparation of the body and the feast. The body of the deceased is then washed with a mixture of special soap, herbs, and water, and is dressed.

THE 3RD DAY

In the morning of the third day, an elaborate feast is prepared in honor of the deceased person. During this feast, people celebrate the person's life and give comfort to the grieving family. The body of the deceased is wrapped in colorful cloth or laid in the casket following the feast. People will come to pay their respects to the deceased person.

THE BURIAL RITE

On the evening of the 4th day before sunset, the body is buried. Various offerings of cowries, flowers, fruits, and food items are given at this time, and on the morning of the fifth day, family members will walk through town asking where the location of the deceased family member is. The villagers will respond that he has gone home.

In conclusion, the Yoruba believe it is crucial to perform all the funeral duties for the soul of the deceased to join the ancestors. It is also very important that the family visit the graves of their family members as well. Some houses or lineages may perform the Itutu ceremony slightly differently however, what we have described here is a brief overview of what is done.

* * *

CHAPTER 12

YORUBA INITIATION RITES AND THE PRIESTLY ROLES

WHAT IS ORISHA INITIATION?

ORISHA INITIATION IS a life-changing experience where a person's head, Ori, is often dedicated to a particular Orisha. The Orisha can then support the person, guiding them through their journey. This process is often referred to as crowning an Orisha. Orisha initiation also consists of receiving an icon of a particular Orisha as well. These ceremonies are often elaborate and may require substantial financial resources due to the expenses involved in acquiring the necessary materials and supporting the priests or priestesses who facilitate the initiation. The rituals often take multiple days to complete and need to be performed by not just one priest but multiple priests as well.

WHY DO PEOPLE GET INITIATED?

Many people seek initiation into Orisha Spirituality for many different personal reasons and needs, including finding a sense of identity, a desire to be in a leadership role, and a belief that initiation will fix many of their problems in life. All these reasons are, in fact, not why someone should get initiated into the Orisha tradition. In fact, these are the wrong reasons to pursue initiation. Let me explain why initiation is not these things.

FINDING A SENSE OF IDENTITY

Discovering who you are and exploring Orisha Spirituality may help you connect with your African ancestors. This is a common reason many people become interested in African Spirituality. Perhaps you have a grandfather who was a Babalawo or a distant relative from Nigeria, motivating you to learn more about Orisha traditions. However, initiation into these traditions won't solve personal issues or problems. As an initiate, you have a significant responsibility to serve the community, which can be exhausting. Priests and priestesses in this tradition must act as role models and make decisions that can profoundly impact people's lives, often under great stress. They serve as intermediaries between the community and the Spirits, and people will seek their guidance on crucial matters, expecting them to provide necessary resources and support. The role of a priest or priestess in Orisha Spirituality is not about serving personal needs but about serving others. I often hear initiates say that if they did not resolve many of their life issues before initiation, they had to do it afterward. Initiation does not magically solve all your life problems. Following initiation, the Orishas may even make your life more difficult, urging you to resolve your personal problems. After initiation, you have a responsibility to serve both the Orishas and the community, and it no longer becomes about you. Those who go into initiation not knowing this often face a rude awakening.

WHY ONE MAY CHOOSE INITIATION

The Orishas may urge a person to get initiated during a consultation or reading to help them stay aligned with their life destiny. The Orishas may require a person to be initiated to avoid a tragedy. The

Orishas may indicate, during a consultation or reading, that initiation is part of a person's destiny, perhaps because they are meant to become a great diviner. In all these instances, it is not the person's decision to get initiated but the Orishas'. Ultimately, the person can choose to opt out of initiation if the Orishas recommend it, but it is never their choice to initiate if the Orishas do not determine the need. It is not the Babalawo's, Iyana's, or any other Orisha priests' decision to give a person the right to be initiated. The Orishas and spirits choose the person, and such recommendations will arise during a reading if this is the case.

Do you need to be initiated to work with Orishas?

No. People can ask favors from an Orisha by leaving a food offering, commonly known as a voluntary Adimu. This can be done at a natural location associated with the Orisha, such as a lake, river, ocean, forest, or mountain, or at a sacred shrine, temple, or the home of a priest or priestess. After making the offering, the person prays to the Orisha for guidance or help. This can be done by anyone, regardless of initiation status. Everyone also has the right to work with their ancestors, Egbe, and Ori. While education is often required to work with these entities, initiation is not necessary. One can learn to use the basic five combinations commonly used in Obí Agbón divination for this purpose. Non-initiates can use this system to communicate with their Ori, ancestors, and Egbe. However, they must be taught by a competent priest, and the obi must be consecrated by a competent priest or priestess for non-initiates to use them. Most non-initiates will receive the Ori ceremony and often have an altar dedicated to their ancestors and a space for their Egbe. Non-initiates primarily work with their ancestors, Ori, and Egbe. They may occasionally visit a river or ocean to make an Adimu offering to an Orisha and make a request.

Orisha initiates not only have to attend to the Orishas and their sacred icons, but also feed them and attend to the needs of the entire community. They must lead the ceremonies and large gatherings, be a good example of moral behavior to the rest of the community, help the community resolve disputes and make crucial decisions in times of famine or threat to the community they serve, help many people in the community who come to them for assistance and guidance, participate in initiations of the people in the community, do marriages, funerals, and birth ceremonies, perform community or individual divinations, and perform the rituals of sacrifice amongst other activities. We are often diviners, healers, the givers of messages from the divine, and many times counselors.

The responsibility of a Priest or Priestess is not one to be taken lightly. It is in many respects a full-time job, and in being such, the Priest or Priestess or Temple often requests a payment of some sort to perform all these tasks and functions. This idea of requesting payment for services is not strange and is often practiced in many other world religions, such as Judaism and Hinduism. It is, however, important for the Priest to be upfront about the prices, and a client seeking services always has the right to get prices from multiple priests if they are not satisfied with the initial cost. A competent, honest priest will charge for only these things. The first being their time and the second being all the resources needed, including the offerings to the various spirits, and the materials needed. In the materials needed the Priest or Priestess may also charge a small material cleaning fee. This provides the materials for the Priest to clean themselves after performing a ritual. A Priest does not charge for Spirituality but for the things mentioned above.

Everything is an exchange of energy, and it is often true that after doing a ritual or a task for a client that consists of consulting the Orishas, the priest is often exhausted from all the energy that was required to do these things. This often requires a large amount of energy to complete these tasks, and we often need to cleanse ourselves as well and replenish this lost energy. The money serves also as an energy exchange, as well as a sacrifice from the client to help the priest take care of himself. Priests often must do consultations/readings for themselves to the Orishas as well as to their Ori and ancestors. The priest often must also make sacrifices for their own sake to the Orishas, so we can continue to be healthy and there for all those who need us. Clients are not alone in this regard. We need to do the same things for ourselves, and sometimes these sacrifices can be way more costly for an initiate than for a non-initiate person. The Orishas expect more out of us in this regard sometimes.

WHY INITIATION MAY NOT ALWAYS BE THE SOLUTION TO YOUR PROBLEMS

As we discussed above, the responsibilities of an initiated priest can be many. It is sadly true that there are way too many people getting initiated by incompetent or corrupt priests seeking financial gain. Initiation is not necessary and is not for everyone. Many people have enough difficulties attending to their ancestors, their Ori, and their daily lives, adding other extra responsibilities by giving people Orishas they may not need is not something a competent community or priest would ever do. Once a person receives an Orisha, they are responsible for taking care of that Orisha for the remainder of their life. This is not something that should be taken lightly! It was common in ancient times for people to go to the temple either once a week or on a specific day dedicated to a particular Orisha. It is at the temple that people can visit and give offerings to the Orishas, either in the form of food or a donation to that Orisha's shrine. Sometimes a priest or several priests may serve a temple, and on various days they may give a sermon or do readings for the public or do a communal ritual where they do readings for several people and all the sacrifices at that time.

In the Orisha tradition, there are several different types of priests. The Babalawo (male) and the Iyanifa (female) are titles given to Ifa priests, while the Babalorisha (male) and Iyalorisha (female) are Orisha priests. Both types of priests are equal, serving different roles, and neither is superior to the other. The notion that one is above the other is a misconception. Babalawo and Iyanifa are titles given to priests initiated into the mysteries of Ifa and are considered priests of the Orisha Orunmila. They have undergone initiation and are crowned with the Orisha Orunmila, signifying their affiliation with the Ifa sect. These priests hold a significant position in the Orisha community, especially in matters of divination. It is believed that Ifa has the final say in any divination-related inquiries.

On the other hand, the Babalorisha (male) and Iyalorisha (female) are priests who have been initiated into other Orishas, excluding Orunmila. While Babalowos and Babalorishas are equally respected among priests, they specialize in different areas. It is common for a Babalorisha to refer a client to a Babalawo if a specific sign arises during a reading, just as a Babalawo might direct a client to a partic- ular Babalorisha if the client needs to receive a specific Orisha that the Babalawo doesn't possess expertise in. The Babalorisha is considered the ultimate authority on the Orisha they have been crowned with, and they are capable of initiating others into that specific Orisha. On the other hand, only a Babalawo has the authority to initiate or give a person the Orisha Orunmila.

* * *

- **Ori Ceremony**: The purpose of this ceremony is to align and honor a person's Ori (individual spiritual essence) through clearing, feeding, and offering homage. It often involves receiving an Ile Ori, a small icon representing the Ori, as a focal point for praise and support.
- **Ancestors' Shrine**: Setting up and consecrating an ancestral shrine is an important initial step in Orisha spirituality. A Babalawo guides the person in honoring their ancestors at the newly created shrine.
- **Honoring Egbe-orun**: The individual receives a small icon to honor their spiritual companions (heavenly mates) and places it in their home.
- **Receiving Elekes**: These beaded necklaces represent specific Orishas and carry their power. They are given to strengthen or protect the wearer, based on consultation results, without requiring full initiation into the Orisha.
- **Receiving Orishas**: Icons representing various Orishas may be received before or after full initiation. They must be cared for and respected.
- **Isefa Ceremony**: This ceremony marks the beginning of a person's journey in Ifá. They receive one hand of Ifá, blessed beads associated with Orunmila, and knowledge of their guardian Orisha (often based on their birth Odu).
- **Crowning (Ocha or Kariocha)**: This initiation ceremony crowns the individual once they know their guardian Orisha, making them a Babalorisha (male) or Iyalorisha (female), a priest or priestess of the specific Orisha.
- **Itá Ceremony**: A ceremony in Ifá that provides guidance and marks the completion of divination.
- **Itéfa Ceremony (Ifá)**: This ceremony follows the Isefa

ceremony and marks the initiation of a person as a priest of Ifá and Orunmila. It represents a full initiation into Ifá.

It is important to note that receiving an Orisha from a priest does not grant the ability to give that Orisha to others unless one is fully initiated to that specific Orisha. For example, a Babalawo can give Orunmila or Eshu, as they are crowned priests of Orunmila, while someone initiated to Obatala can give Obatala to others, and so on.

* * *

It is important for Orisha Initiates and devotees to observe the following and not break these taboos:

1. Respect your parents and express gratitude to them.
2. Show respect to the elders in your community.
3. Be kind to the poor and less fortunate.
4. Maintain hope and positivity for the future.
5. Do not use your power and authority to harm others.
6. Respect the earth and the environment.
7. Avoid immoral behavior, including stealing, lying, cheating, murder, and drug use.
8. Always respect the Orisha, perform your ebos, and follow their guidance.

* * *

THE ROLE AND RESPONSIBILITIES OF A PRIEST

The role of Orisha Priests in Yoruba tradition is often multifaceted and requires many responsibilities, including the following:

- **Preservation and Guarding of Yoruba Culture and Orisha Tradition:** Orisha Priests play a vital role in preserving and safeguarding the Yoruba tribe's culture and the sacred traditions associated with the Orishas. They ensure that the knowledge, rituals, and history are passed down to future generations, maintaining the cultural identity of the community.

- **Serving the Orishas:** Orisha Priests act as intermediaries between the human community and the Orishas, serving the deities and fulfilling their needs. They conduct ceremonies, make offerings, and perform rituals to honor and appease the Orishas, maintaining a harmonious relationship between the spiritual realm and the community.
- **Providing Guidance and Divination:** Orisha Priests possess the ability to communicate with the Orishas and divine the causes of problems or difficulties faced by individuals or the community, offering insights and guidance to navigate life's challenges.
- **Healing and Spiritual Support:** Priests often serve as the spiritual Doctors of the community and often possess knowledge of traditional Yoruba medicine, which they use to heal illnesses.
- **Social Leadership and Conflict Resolution:** Orisha Priests assume a crucial role in maintaining social order and harmony within the community. They act as mediators in disputes, assisting in conflict resolution and fostering reconciliation. Their wisdom and spiritual insights contribute to the well-being of the community as they guide individuals towards virtuous and ethical conduct.
- **Participation in Community Events:** Orisha Priests actively lead and participate in religious ceremonies, festivals, and rituals. They ensure the continuity of the spiritual connection between the living and the ancestral spirits, honoring and caring for the ancestors. Through their

involvement, they strengthen the communal bonds and perpetuate the rich cultural traditions of the Yoruba people.

In summary, Orisha Priests, such as the Babalawos and Babalorishas, hold significant spiritual positions within the Yoruba tradition. They serve as healers, diviners, spiritual guides, social leaders, and custodians of the cultural heritage. Their role is crucial in maintaining the balance between the human and spiritual realms, providing support, and upholding the sacred traditions of the community.

* * *

CHAPTER 13

IWA-PELE AND OMOLUABI

IWA-PELE IS a fundamental concept in Yoruba spiritual tradition and can be translated to mean "good character" or "gentle character," and it is a core value that governs the beliefs and practices of the Yoruba people. Iwa-pele is seen as the foundation for living a fulfilling life, and it is believed that having good character is essential for achieving success and happiness in all aspects of life. Yoruba religion teaches that Iwa-pele is not only important for individuals, but also for communities, as it promotes social harmony, cooperation, and respect for others. The concept of Iwa-pele is closely tied to the idea of Ori, which refers to an individual's inner consciousness or personal destiny. According to Yoruba religion, Ori is the guiding force behind an individual's actions and choices, and having good character is essential for fulfilling one's destiny and achieving spiritual growth. Yoruba religion also emphasizes the importance of cultivating good character through daily practice and self-reflection.

By practicing self-reflection, we can strengthen our connection with our Ori and become better equipped to navigate life's challenges and achieve our goals. In addition to personal practice, Yoruba religion also emphasizes the importance of community support in cultivating Iwa-pele. This includes participating in communal rituals and ceremonies, seeking guidance from elders and spiritual leaders, and working together to promote social harmony and justice. Overall, the concept of Iwa-pele is a foundational value in Yoruba religion that emphasizes the importance of good character in achieving spiritual growth, personal fulfillment, and social harmony. By cultivating Iwa-pele through daily practice and community support, individuals can live a more meaningful and fulfilling life in accordance with their Ori and the greater good of their community. In the Yoruba tradition, the concept of Iwa-pele, or "good or gentle character," is seen as an essential part of this path. When we embody Iwa-pele, we become what the Yoruba call **Omoluabi,** which means to be upright and virtuous.

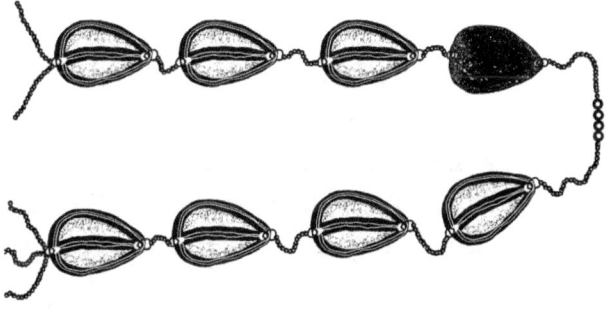

The image above is of an Opele Chain, which is commonly used by Babalawos during divination and is seen as a symbol of balance. It is believed that Iwa Pele can bring balance to a person's life and help bring the person into ire or alignment with their destiny. On one side of the coin, we have divination and sacrifice, and on the other side, we have Iwa Pele and a person's character. It is believed that these are the main components that keep a person in ire during their life.

* * *

Iwa-pele is sometimes described as a list of positive ethical principles of virtue that we should strive daily in our lives to practice, such as treating others with respect and compassion, having self-control, and being patient. Iwa-pele might be described at other times as avoiding various types of bad behavior, such as avoiding becoming greedy, envious, avoiding dishonesty, impatience, and anger. The Yoruba also have this concept called "tutu," akin to coolness, referring to one's composure and moral conduct during challenging situations. It implies maintaining a calm and composed demeanor amidst life's unpredictability. Tutu suggests that while one may not control every aspect of life, individuals can control their reactions to it.

The Yoruba value the idea of being calm and collected, considering it the optimal way to navigate societal interactions. This notion of "tutu" emphasizes possessing composure and a level-headed approach in facing life's challenges. Within Yoruba society, being cool-headed is not just desirable but deemed necessary, especially among those with higher prestige. Iwa-pele may also be described by some Orisha communities as the obligation to follow one's taboos and prohibitions that are given during divination, as well as honoring both one's ancestors, the Orishas, and the elders of the community.

What constitutes Iwa-pele may differ from community to community, but it is important that you have a basic understanding of the concept in Orisha spirituality. During a divination reading, the Orishas may reveal to us that we may need to change our own behavior or character, and at that time offer us guidance through their priests, Babalawos, Babalorishas, Iyanifas, etc. The Orishas may also, during a reading, offer us guidance on how to cultivate the virtues of Iwa-Pele to overcome obstacles and achieve success in our lives, especially if we are lacking in certain moral behavior or virtue, which could be preventing us from achieving our spiritual milestones in life.

.   .   .

In conclusion, may we continue to live in a way that pleases the Orishas, Olodumare, and our ancestors. May the Orishas and our Ori continue to guide us in a direction of self-growth, transformation, and in a way that ultimately brings us peace, abundance, and ire in our lives.

* * *

COMMUNICATING
WITH THE SPIRITS

PART 2

CHAPTER 14
INTRODUCTION TO DIVINATION

DIVINATION SERVES as the cornerstone of Orisha spirituality, acting as the conduit through which practitioners and devotees establish direct communication with their deceased ancestors, as well as with the Orishas. Divination provides insights into helping practitioners address their worldly challenges and gives them a road map to follow so they can continue to align themselves with their destiny here on earth.

Divination in Yoruba spirituality is seen as a form of spirit communication and is natural and unique to every individual who seeks the guidance of those ancestors who reside in the spirit world. There is a belief amongst the Yoruba that the Orishas taught humans to use divination, and that divination has always existed, even in heaven, since the beginning. It is said that the Orisha Orunmila came to earth during ancient times, during the existence of the Kingdom of Ile Ife, and taught his disciples how to consult Odu Ifá here on earth to help us spiritually survive and evolve here. There are many stories of Orunmila on earth as a diviner described within the Odu Ifá literary corpus. Many stories are also passed from family to family and community to community and have not been published or written down as well.

The Odu Ifá consists of 16 large parts, each with 16 subsets or Ese (stories), making a total of 256. Each Odu is believed to be a unique pattern or signature created by the divination tool when used during a divination session. This pattern is created by dropping the tool on the ground. Once the pattern presents itself, it is believed that it creates a unique energy. The Yoruba traditionalists believe that these Odu are the most basic energy building blocks that all things in the universe arose out of. This is to say, these energies or patterns are believed to be the original energies of the natural world that Olodumare (God) put into existence, and from their combination with each other arose all the forces that govern nature today.

The best way to understand this is by equating the 256 odus to a sort of description of all the cosmic energies in the universe, like the periodic table to elements that is often found on the wall in a high school chemistry class. The primary purpose of divination is to reconnect to our heavenly consciousness and align ourselves with our ultimate purpose. It is through sacrifice that we overcome our difficulties and achieve our goals.

THE PURPOSE OF DIVINATION AND SPIRIT COMMUNICATION IN YORUBA SPIRITUALITY

1. **Providing Spiritual Healing**: Consulting the Orishas through Divination can aid in identifying various spiritual imbalances and negative energies that may need to be addressed in our lives, so we can live more spiritually enriched. Divination often reveals sacrifices needed to rebalance energies that are out of harmony with one's nature and destiny on earth.
2. **Communication with Ancestors and Orishas**: We believe that divination provides a direct connection with the

ancestors and Orishas, who assist and support us on our earthly journey.

3. **Gaining Insight into the Future**: Orisha practitioners use divination to gain insight into the future, helping them prepare for upcoming challenges or opportunities.

4. **Aiding Decision-Making**: It is common for Orisha practitioners to use divination to guide their decisions in various life circumstances. Divination helps determine if a chosen path aligns with the practitioner's spiritual destiny. Many practitioners consult the Orishas or their ancestors before making significant life decisions.

5. **A Spiritual Connection**: The foundation of Orisha Spirituality is the belief that we can communicate with ancestors even after they have passed away, and that death is not the end. This belief provides strength and healing for both individuals and communities.

* * *

Divination is essential to the survival of the Orisha tradition and is what makes the Orisha tradition unique and dynamic. Unlike many other religions, we have the ability to receive answers from the Orishas through divination. Divination serves as an essential bridge that connects the living to the world of the spirits. It is not only believed to be necessary for the Yoruba but essential for all of humanity for us to gain insight into our own spiritual development here on earth. It is the responsibility of the ancestors to guide us and watch over us during our lives. Divination serves as an essential way we can continue to engage with our ancestors, which, for the traditional Yorubas, is a necessary aspect of all human life here on earth.

The diviner serves as an intermediary between the Spirits and the person coming for a reading. A diviner is often in a position of authority within their community. Diviners tend to be initiated Priests and Priestesses who are then taught the art of divination by another elder priest or priestess before obtaining permission to serve the public as a diviner. Becoming a diviner within the Orisha tradition often takes years of practice and intense training to acquire the skills to work, serve, and communicate with different spirits, each of whom has a unique personality and temperament.

A diviner plays a crucial role in the community, carrying ethical and moral responsibilities. We have a responsibility to assist those who come to us, even if it means directing them to another diviner or house. Clients and people who come to us often regard us as examples to be emulated within the Ifá and Orisha tradition. A diviner should never attempt to harm, take advantage of, manipulate, or coerce a client. Engaging in such actions not only violates the moral and ethical responsibilities of a diviner when working with the public but also violates the laws of nature. A good diviner will often be humble. One simple rule to follow is "Do no harm." We are the messengers between the client and the spirits; we are not the message.

A client's business in a reading is also not our business. The best way to do our job is by conveying the message the Orishas want the client to hear. Our goal is to simply convey what the divinities want to tell the client. As diviners, we should always recognize that a client has rights. We can emphasize to them, for example, that performing their sacrifices is important and should be completed, but ultimately, the client always has the right to object or seek the help or advice of another person. Our goal, again, is to do no harm and assist them to the best of our abilities in their own spiritual journey.

Clients often look up to us for answers. We must always strive to be good role models and adhere to good character (Iwa-Pele) when in the public eye. Here is a list of some ethical responsibilities we have towards our clients:

- **Honesty and Integrity**: The diviner should provide an honest and accurate reading to the best of their abilities, refraining from false information or misleading interpretations. Clearly communicating the cost of the reading and any additional services, ensuring transparency in financial matters.
- **Confidentiality**: Respecting the client's privacy by keeping the details of the reading and any personal information shared during the session confidential.
- **Empathy and Compassion**: Demonstrating empathy and compassion towards the client's concerns and questions, regardless of the nature of the reading.
- **Informed Consent**: Clearly explaining the process and purpose of the divination, ensuring that the client understands what to expect and agrees to proceed. A diviner should never attempt to read someone without asking for permission first.
- **Objectivity:** Striving to remain objective and not imposing personal biases, judgments, or opinions onto the reading.
- **Ethical Boundaries:** Maintaining professional and ethical boundaries, refraining from exploiting the client's vulnerability or dependence.
- **Follow-up Support:** If necessary, offering support or additional resources to the client for further exploration or assistance in addressing their concerns.

1. *Feeding and taking care of the Orishas and other spirits.*
2. *Giving the spirits respect and appreciation.*
3. *Approaching the spirits with a humble heart.*
4. *The diviner also has a responsibility to take care of him or herself by performing the necessary sacrifices needed to clean and align themselves from sickness.*

In conclusion, divination is the core of Orisha spirituality; it connects practitioners to their ancestors and the Orishas, allowing them to receive insight, knowledge, guidance, and healing from them. Diviners hold a special role and are held in high regard by the community they serve. Because of this, Diviners should always adhere to the ethical and professional standards of the profession of the priesthood. They should always serve those who come to them in a neutral, non-judgmental, and respectful way.

* * *

CHAPTER 15

UNDERSTANDING ÌFÁ

UNDERSTANDING ODU ÌFÁ

IFÁ IS a sophisticated system of divination within Yoruba spirituality, governed by the Orisha Òrúnmìlà. The term *Ifá* refers both to the divination system and to the sacred corpus of knowledge it contains, known as *Odu Ifá*. In English, Ifá can be understood as "the divine wisdom and voice of Olódùmarè (God)." More culturally, *Odu Ifá* is a collection of knowledge, stories, taboos, and wisdom passed down orally through generations by the Yoruba people. The art of divination is considered sacred and is used to seek guidance from the Orishas. In Ifá, divination specifically seeks the counsel of Òrúnmìlà, the Orisha of divine wisdom and destiny, who resides over the sacred Ifá. Òrúnmìlà guides the Babaláwo, the Ifá priest and diviner, in interpreting the Odu.

THE PROCESS OF IFA DIVINATION

The Ifá divination process uses either sacred palm nuts (*ikin*) from the '*Elaeis guineensis*' tree, or a divining chain called an *opelé*. The *opelé* consists of eight pieces of coconut or seed pods, often called *Aguntan*, from the *'Schrebera arborea'* tree. These eight pieces generate 256 possible combinations (16 × 16), each corresponding to a specific Odu. The Yoruba word *Odu* literally means "womb" or "basket," but in Ifá it refers to a "chapter" or unit of sacred knowledge. Metaphysically, an Odu is composed of Àshe, forming an energy matrix, a dynamic pattern of creative force that flows through existence.

This energy manifests in the world, shaping events, circumstances, and individual destinies. It is the raw creative energy of the universe, comparable to elements in chemistry, forming the foundation of life and cosmic order. During divination, the Babaláwo often transcribes the Odu onto a circular wooden board called the *òpón Ifá*, a central tool in Ifá practice. The *òpón Ifá* symbolizes the entire universe.

The Babaláwo may also interpret the Odu based on the way the divination tools land on a sacred mat. For the Yoruba, the Orishas are as real as the people around us, and divination is a direct connection to the divine. Each Odu contains a vast body of sacred knowledge: stories, Yoruba history, verses, medicinal practices, moral teachings, and guidance associated with specific Orishas. Receiving an Odu provides direction in life, including:

- **Actions to avoid (taboos)**
- **Sacrifices (ẹbọ) or rituals to appease the Orishas or correct an imbalance**
- **Guidance on honoring and connecting with ancestors**
- **Remedies for illness or spiritual afflictions in the form of medicinal herbs or ritual practices**
- **Ways to strengthen one's Ashe (spiritual power)**
- **Advice for maintaining harmony with natural and cosmic forces (àdán)**
- **Guidance on moral conduct, ethical behavior, and maintaining spiritual balance**

The Yoruba believe that the Odu not only offers guidance for earthly life but also contains the secrets of creation and the mysteries of existence. In Yoruba cosmology, an Odu is more than a sacred text; it is a living language through which humans and divinities communicate with each other. At birth, each person is born under a specific life Odu, a unique energetic signature that serves as a divine blueprint for their existence. This Odu, or divine pattern of *Ashe*, is the source of a person's spiritual power and divine energy, dictating how the person can manifest their spiritual power into the physical world. Though we may not remember our life Odu, its energy is ever-present, shaping our experiences, opportunities, and challenges.

Knowing one's Odu allows alignment with this inherent energy, illuminates purpose, and offers protection from both spiritual and material harm. Through initiation into the Orisha tradition and the sacred act of divination, this divine signature is fully revealed, awakening the individual to their destiny and enabling them to consciously move in harmony with the cosmic flow of existence.

INTERPRETING THE ODU IFA

During divination, the Babaláwo begins by invoking Òrúnmìlà and ritually manipulating the sacred palm nuts (*ikin*). Through this precise method, a specific Odu is revealed, a distinct pattern of divine knowledge and destiny. Once identified, the Babaláwo carefully transcribes the markings of the Odu onto the ifa board (opon) using a sacred powder called *Iyerosun,* made from a termite-eaten wood dust of the Iyerosun tree. The marks are a codified visual language, preserving the spiritual signature of the revealed Odu. The Babaláwo then decodes and interprets the Odu, drawing on years of training and memorization. Every Odu contains numerous verses (*ese Ifá*), proverbs, historical narratives, moral teachings, and ritual instructions.

The interpretation guides the client, indicating warnings, recommended sacrifices (*ebo*), or spiritual alignments needed for their life circumstances. The photo below shows two traditional examples of how an Odu is transcribed during an Ifá consultation, highlighting the precise and symbolic nature of this sacred divination system.

* * *

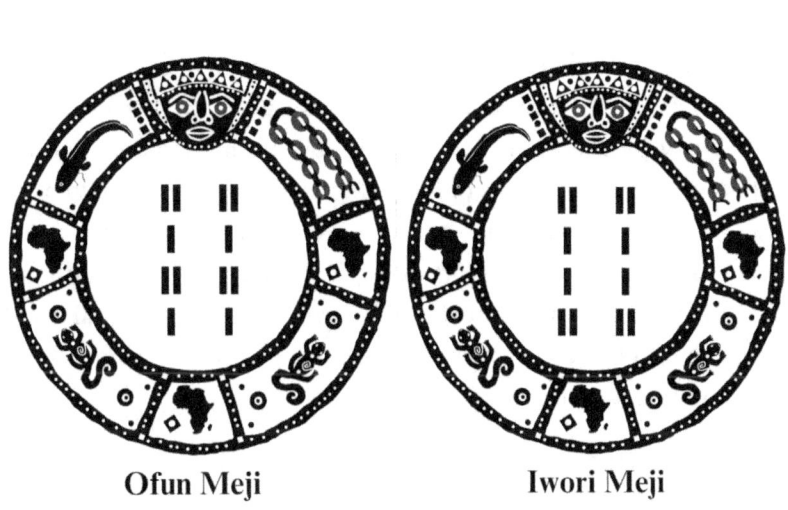

Ofun Meji   Iwori Meji

As shown in the image above, each Odu, such as (*Iwori Meji*) and (*Ofun Meji*), is depicted with eight lines, four on each side, forming two "legs." An Odu must have both legs to be complete. The right leg represents masculine energy, while the left leg represents feminine energy. Some Ifá priests interpret the right, masculine side as reflecting the external, macrocosmic energies, and the left, feminine side as representing the internal, microcosmic energies. Together, these two legs create a distinctive energy signature within the sacred vessel of creation, known as *Igba Iwa*. The lines of an Odu represent the flow of Ashe, the divine life force. A single line (I) symbolizes blessings, illumination, and open energy, while a double line (II) indicates closure, stagnation, or blocked energy. In this way, an Odu functions as both a roadmap and a map of energetic patterns, representing the forces that govern nature, human life, and the universe. Writing an Odu in this form helps visualize and interpret these unique energy signatures.

UNDERSTANDING ESE IFA

Each Odu is again divided into verses, known as *Ese*. Every Odu contains a vast number of *Ese*, though there is no exact count, and no single written source encompasses them all. Much of this knowledge is still transmitted orally, and over time, additional legends and stories may be incorporated into the Ifá corpus. It is common to encounter slight variations of well-known stories from one community to another, so hearing multiple versions of the same tale is normal. This is why it is important to follow the specific traditions of your Orisha community, lineage, or house. A competent Babalawo or Iyanifa should be able to recite at least two verses for each of the 256 Odus, totaling a minimum of 512 verses.

* * *

THE TOOLS OF IFA

When you consult an Ifá priest for a reading, you will often see a variety of tools used in the divination process. The most common tools include the *òpón Ifá* (divination tray), *iyeròsùn* powder, the *opelé* chain, *iroké Ifá* (divining tapper), *irukere*(fly whisk), and the *ikin* (Sacred palm nuts).

The Opon Ifa is commonly known as a divination tray or Ifa board. These trays are typically crafted from wood sourced from the African Iroko tree (Milicia excelsa). Artisans skilled in their carving often create them, although occasionally Opons are made from less costly woods due to the high price of Iroko. The opon serves as a tool for divination using sacred palm nuts in the context of the Orisha spiritual tradition. It is a symbolic miniature representation of the cosmic universe and is often adorned with carvings reflecting Yoruba mythology. Often, on the top of the board is a carving of a face representing the Orisha Eshu, who is seen as an intermediary. Eshu often opens the doors and facilitates communication between the babalawo and Ifa, as well as communication between the babalawo and the other Orishas. Eshu is always honored and given offerings following every consultation. The opon can be divided into five sections: top, bottom, left, right, and center, as seen in the image above. Each quadrant represents the four major cardinal directions and the four cosmic movements of existence.

The left side of the Opon symbolizing the west is often referred to as the **Osi-Opon** and is sometimes represented by the Odu *Oyeku*, which symbolizes transitions, the end of a cycle, change, death, and transformation.

The right side of the opon, called **Otun-Opon,** sometimes represented as the Odu Eji-Ogbe, symbolizes expanding light, east, new beginnings, and transformation, urging the need to embrace what lies ahead and move forward.

The top of the Opon, called **Ori-Opon,** often symbolizes the spiritual aspects of ourselves, the divinities, and heavenly realms. The center point of the opon, called (**kádàrá**), means fate in English; this point symbolizes clarity, one's path, and destiny.

The center often represents the central point, connecting all the sections together, symbolizing the natural balance we continue to maintain on our spiritual path and the bottom of the opon called **Ese-Opon** often represents the physical realm of earth and material existence, emphasizing our material well-being and earthly challenges.

In summary, the opon or ifa board within Yoruba spirituality often represents our flow through life and death, spiritual and physical transformation, and serves as a sort of microcosm of the entire universe. When we use Obi, one can determine what aspect of life the Obi is talking about based on the location on the Opon-Ifa board, where the Obi pieces land after tossing them.

Other tools in Ifa include: the Iyerosun powder, Opele chain, Iroke Ifa, and Irukere, each playing a crucial role in the intricate process of divination, facilitating communication with the orishas and providing guidance in matters of life, destiny, and spirituality. Below is a more detailed description of these tools:

Iyerosun Powder

Iyerosun is a sacred powder often used to mark Odu on the opon ifa during divination using sacred palm nuts. In Africa, Iyerosun powder originates from the termites that ingest the wood from a particular tree unique for this purpose. In the Caribbean, the powder is often derived through other traditional means, such as yams. Iyerosun is scattered onto the Opon-Ifa (Divination tray) and spread across its surface to mark the Odu Ifa.

Opele Chain

Opele is a chain used by Ifa priests (Babalawos) for divination. It is often made from either coconut pieces or traditional African seeds from either the *Schrebera arborea* tree or the Egbere seed. The opele consists of eight pieces of either seed or coconut pieces tied together. It serves as a faster method for determining Odu during divination rather than the slower process of utilizing the sacred palm nuts. The diviner will determine the Odu by throwing the Opele, and the Odu pattern is often interpreted from this.

Iroke Ifa

Iroke, also called the Ifa divination tapper, resembles a tusk of an animal with carved images in it. Traditionally, they were made of ivory, but today they are often made of wood or deer antlers. The Iroke is used by the Babalawo or the Ifa diviner to tap rhythmically on the opon ifa to establish a link from the physical realm to the spiritual realm in heaven to open communication so the diviner can better receive messages and guidance.

The Irukere, also known as a fly whisk, is a sacred tool intricately crafted from horsehair or other materials and often embellished with beads. Beyond its symbolic significance, this implement serves a spiritual purpose, expelling negative energies from the diviner and cleansing spaces of spiritual impurities. More than a mere fly swatter, the Irukere holds spiritual power, establishing a connection with the Orishas. It plays a vital role in practices such as cleansing, purification, and channeling positive energy and *Ase* within the Ifa divination system and the broader Yoruba culture.

The Irukere is frequently employed to clear sacred spaces, homes, and places of worship of bad energy. In Yoruba culture, chiefs and other authoritative figures are sometimes seen as having an Irokere in their possession. Each of these items plays a crucial role in the intricate process of Ifa divination, offering a means for communication with the Orisha and providing guidance in matters of life, destiny, and spirituality.

Next, we will discuss the 16 major Odu ifa ...

* * *

THE SIXTEEN MAJOR ODUS
OF IFA AND THEIR DESCRIPTIONS

* * *

Ogbe Meji

Eji-Ogbe embodies themes of light, creation, clarity, destiny, and alignment with the Ori. Its energy represents the original light from which all things emerge, symbolizing the limitless potential of the first spark of creation. In divination, Eji-Ogbe reflects all that is visible and known, similar to Alafia in Obi divination. Unlike any other sign, it contains only light, free from darkness, representing clear vision and effortless progress toward goals. This is a time when blessings and meaningful opportunities flow, aligning with one's true potential.

Oyeku Meji

Oyeku Meji embodies the principle of darkness, being the sole sign where no light exists, symbolizing complete darkness and the absence of the spark of creation. It represents the unknown and signifies the end of something, contrasting Ogbe's representation of beginnings and known entities. Oyeku parallels the natural life cycle, where all things have both a start and a finish. Just as attempting to revive a lifeless plant is often futile, encountering Oyeku may indicate the necessity to move on from a situation that has reached its end. It signifies the darkness surrounding the light, representing the transition between each divine spark (Ogbe). In divination, Oyeku indicates death and the transition from one phase to another. The ancestors often speak when this Odu appears in a reading.

Iwori Meji

The essence of Iwori Meji is frequently characterized as a force guiding the transition and change occurring as we navigate between the visible (light) and the unseen (darkness). Representing our inner metamorphosis. Iwori helps us to transform into something new, with surprises. Iwori mirrors the changes within us, fostering potential spiritual growth. Just like the metamorphosis a caterpillar undergoes to become a butterfly, Iwori is the dynamic energy propelling us from one state to another. Despite its occasional unpredictability and chaos, Iwori Meji holds the potential for spiritual growth. Iwori's energy helps to transform us into something better as we evolve on the journey of our lives. The emergence of Iwori Meji frequently suggests the person possesses great potential, yet these opportunities fail to materialize due to flaws in their character. Iwori Meji often provides insights into the individual's inner nature.

Odi Meji

The energy of Odi Meji is often seen as the energy of reproduction and birth. It talks about the relationship between both the male and female polarities and the balance needed between these two opposites to complete the task of bringing forth new life into the world. When this Odu comes up, it often talks about the importance of stability and being grounded in life. When Odi Meji comes up in divination, it often points to establishing or maintaining connections and having a strong, stable foundation in one's life. This Odu also points to possible renewal and regeneration. In the negative, this Odu can signify either the deterioration of one's stable connections in life, or it may point to conflict within the family unit, or it may point to excessive rigidity and the need to try a new direction.

* * *

Irosun Meji

Irosun embodies the wisdom of the ancestors, generational consciousness, and the shaping of destiny through lineage. Its energy emphasizes patience, persistence, and disciplined effort, reminding us that meaningful goals are rarely achieved without hard work, humility, and honesty. This Odu calls for strong character, discernment of illusion from reality, and clarity of thought. Irosun points to the importance of honoring the head (*ori*), the seat of wisdom, memory, and mental faculties. The bird Osun symbolizes this guidance, acting as a sacred messenger to the Orishas and to Olodumare. When Irosun appears, it encourages looking to one's ancestors for support and guidance, practicing gratitude for what we already have, and recognizing the value of sacrifice to ease life's challenges. This Odu reminds us that success comes through diligence and integrity. We must live for our own destiny, not someone else's, and work persistently to achieve it. While life may not be easy under Irosun's energy, through patience, sacrifice, and dedication, our goals and true destiny can be realized.

155

Owonrin Meji

Owonrin Meji embodies the energy of crossroads, change, and adaptability. It reminds us that life is unpredictable, and the outcomes we experience are shaped by our choices and actions. This Odu teaches the principle of balance between scarcity and abundance: just as a farmer cannot harvest more than what he has planted, we reap the results of the effort, intention, and energy we put into our lives. When Owonrin Meji appears, it signals the importance of being mindful of our actions and maintaining balance in all areas of life. It emphasizes that our present behavior and decisions determine our future circumstances. Adaptability, patience, and foresight are key under this energy, guiding us through life's uncertainties while showing that what we sow through work, integrity, and intention is ultimately what we will receive.

Obara Meji

Obara Meji represents the power of perspective and the ability to transform one's life. This Odu teaches that how we see things shapes our experiences and our capacity to grow. It calls us to rise above distractions, embrace change, and pursue larger goals with clarity. The symbol of Obara Meji shows light at the top and darkness at the bottom: the light signifies insight, new understanding, and the potential for abundance, while the darkness represents the old ways and limitations we must leave behind. Through this Odu, we learn that true transformation comes from seeing reality as it is, allowing us to turn scarcity into wealth and cultivate material and spiritual abundance in all areas of life.

Okanran Meji

Okanran Meji talks about facing our emotions and feelings that can either help us or hinder us. This Odu teaches us that we need to integrate the heart (Okan) with our rational side and our intuition to maintain alignment in our destiny. Okanran advises against radical, emotionally charged decisions without first thinking them through. Okanran is also associated with the balance of emotions and rationality when making decisions. This Odu underscores balance as crucial for progress, cautioning against uncontrolled emotions or a lack of emotions. The keyword here is balance. Okanran Meji highlights the importance of progressing through life's challenges with strength and commitment to goals. It delves into the impact of emotions, emphasizing the necessity to balance and control them during difficulties. This Odu teaches the integration of the heart (Okan) with rationality and intuition before making decisions. Okanran cautions against impulsive, emotionally charged decisions, promoting thoughtful actions and self-judgment. Okanran suggests considering all points of view before deciding.

*   *   *

Ogunda Meji

Ogunda Meji embodies the energy of iron and war, representing the force that drives action, courage, and progress. This Odu teaches us to confront challenges directly, cutting through obstacles and clearing the paths that allow growth and advancement. Guided by Ogun, the Orisha of iron, war, technology, and labor, Ogunda emphasizes that nothing worthwhile is achieved without hard work, discipline, and determination. While some Odu, like Okanran Meji, focus on emotional balance, Ogunda calls for physical willpower and persistence, urging us to meet life's trials with courage and strength. Ogun both tests and empowers us, showing that the effort we put into overcoming obstacles transforms struggle into strength. Ogunda Meji reminds us that progress and success require action: the forge of life's challenges strengthens the heart, builds resilience, and clears the way for lasting achievement.

* * *

Osa Meji

When Osa Meji shows up, it often signifies a sudden, unexpected change. The dominant orisha in this odu is Oya. Some things in life happen very suddenly and quickly, and they may not be fair or pleasant. The Orisha Oya primarily rules this Odu. Oya rules the force of nature that brings sudden and abrupt changes in people's lives, especially if something needs to change in that person's life. However, she does give a lot of warning before-hand! It is important we trust our intuition. This change can often be felt as distressing and chaotic, but following it comes new beginnings, renewal, and growth. Sometimes Oya will present in people's lives like a whirlwind because the person has not addressed an aspect of their life in need of change. Other times, Oya will present herself in someone's life as a fierce protector, defending the person from harm. Oya is also seen as a great protector of the dead and the ancestors and is the mother of Egungun. Sometimes, Egungun may also speak when this Odu appears.

* * *

Ika Meji

Ika Meji talks about the importance of harnessing our inner power and building up the personal *ashe* we possess within to direct it towards the positive manifestations we want in our lives. Ika Meji also talks about the accumulation of personal Ashe to achieve desired goals. When Ika Meji appears in the negative manifestation, it warns us against using our own personal power in a self-destructive way. It also warns us to avoid the things in life that can drain us of our personal power. We should avoid giving our personal power to others so freely. It is believed by the Yoruba that the loss of personal power can result in physical and spiritual illness. Ashe is seen as a reward we receive from the divinities for doing certain things correctly here on earth. Such things may include possessing good character, doing good deeds, and making *ebo* after divination. In conclusion, Ika Meji brings with it the blessings of accomplishment and healing if we build up our own inner Ashe and learn how to move positively towards our goals.

* * *

Oturupon Meji

Oturupon Meji signals a focus on health, endurance, and stability. This Odu reminds us that taking care of the body is essential for navigating life's challenges. It encourages proper nutrition, attention to spiritual practices or taboos, stress management, and safeguarding the immune system to prevent illness before it arises. Oturupon Meji also emphasizes resilience and perseverance. Life may bring difficulties, but by caring for yourself steadily and mindfully, you build the strength to endure and overcome hardships. In some cases, healing may involve rituals, sacrifices, or cleansing practices to restore balance and clear obstacles. This Odu advises practical action: it is a good time for a medical checkup or consulting a healthcare professional if something feels off. By combining mindful self-care, preventative measures, and spiritual awareness, Oturupon Meji helps maintain physical, emotional, and spiritual stability, allowing you to face life's trials with endurance and confidence.

Otura Meji

Otura Meji often grants the ability to perceive truth and experience visions. These visions may arise from dreams, spiritual sources, or align with deeply held beliefs about the world. On the downside, these visions might foster a sense of inflated importance, moral superiority, or rigidness, hindering personal growth. In a positive light, Otura's visions can assist individuals in personal development and goal achievement. Teaching others can be challenging if one lacks the knowledge of the subject.

Irete Meji

Irete Meji serves as a reminder of the power of personal integrity and virtuous living. This Odu warns against self-sabotage and impulsive, harmful choices, guiding us instead toward paths that build strength of character. It highlights that true wealth, fortune, and blessings come through perseverance, good conduct, and moral discipline. Initiation and spiritual guidance from Ifá and the Orishas are emphasized as tools for personal growth and self-improvement. By cultivating virtue, honoring commitments, and acting with honesty, one aligns with the forces that bring lasting blessings. In some cases, sacrifices or rituals may be required to remove obstacles and protect life, reinforcing the importance of persistence and determination. Irete Meji teaches that blessings are earned through integrity: living with honor and building good character opens the way for prosperity, guidance, and fulfillment in life.

Oshe Meji

When Oshe Meji appears, it highlights the importance of patience and thoughtful deliberation before taking action. This Odu teaches that true abundance and prosperity arise when decisions are made with care and timing is respected. By pausing to consider all options, one aligns with the natural flow of creativity and wealth, allowing opportunities to unfold fully. Oshe Meji reminds us that blessings manifest most powerfully when actions harmonize with the rhythm of the universe, and that waiting for the right moment can invite greater prosperity, creative insight, and lasting success

* * *

Ofun Meji

Ofun Meji, the final Odu among the 16 major Ifá Odus, marks the completion of a cycle. It signals a time when efforts and experiences reach their fulfillment, bringing the lessons of the journey into focus. This Odu illuminates the path with clarity and understanding, revealing truths that were once hidden and showing the way forward with transparency. It is a moment of emergence into light, where challenges are resolved, and obstacles give way to insight and wisdom. In divination, Ofun Meji calls for reflection and discernment, encouraging one to embrace spiritual growth, act with integrity, and align actions with truth. It reminds us that the end of one cycle is the beginning of greater illumination, and that understanding comes when we fully integrate the lessons of experience.

Learning the sixteen major Odù Ifá can be hard at first, but using memory tools like short phrases and poems makes it easier. A mnemonic is a tool that links information to words or patterns to help you remember it. For the Odù, each phrase connects key words to specific Odù, helping you recall both their order and meaning. Two simple phrases can help: *"**Orishas orchestrate infinite opportunities in offering Obi, Okra, Orogbo**"* covers the first nine Odù, and *"**Oya is open to increasing one's opportunities**"* covers the last seven. Breaking the Odù into these two groups makes them much easier to memorize.

- *Phrase One:* "Orishas orchestrate infinite opportunities in offering Obi, Okra, Orogbo."

1. **Orishas:** (*OGBE*)
2. **Orchestrate:** (*OYEKU*)
3. **Infinite:** (*IWORI*)
4. **Opportunities:** (*ODI*)
5. **In:** (*IROSUN*)
6. **Offering:** (*OWONRIN*)
7. **Obi:** (*OBARA*)
8. **Okra**: (*OKANRAN*)
9. **Orogbo**: (*OGUNDA*)

- *Phrase Two:* "Oya is open to increasing one's opportunities,"

10. **Oya:** (*OSA*)
11. **Is:** (*IKA*)
12. **Open:** (*OTURUPON*)
13. **To:** (*OTURA*)

14. **Increasing:** (*IRETE*)
15. **One's:** (*OSHE*)
16. **Opportunities:** (*OFUN*)

Using these two mnemonic phrases makes learning the order of the sixteen Odù simple and easy to remember.

* * *

CHAPTER 16

THE YORUBA CONCEPT OF SACRIFICE

IF YOU HAVE EVER UNDERGONE a divination reading within the Orisha tradition, you have probably observed that a sacrifice or "Ebo" is typically recommended afterward. Let's commence this chapter with a fundamental question: what is sacrifice, and how frequently must we make sacrifices to accomplish our goals in life? Many aspects of life involve sacrifice. For instance, dedicating an hour daily to walking and exercising to enhance your health or practicing financial prudence by saving money and reducing spending, either to secure a better retirement or to finally take that dream vacation you've always yearned for.

These are just a couple of the myriad sacrifices we make in our daily lives. In Yoruba tradition, it is held that sacrifice brings blessings, often referred to as *"Ire,"* into one's life. The Yoruba regard sacrifice as one of the most significant facets of existence, viewing it to enhance an individual's "Ase" or power. There exists a belief that everyone possesses a certain amount of power, known as "Ase," enabling them to manifest their desires, provided it aligns with their destinies and is approved by the divinities and ancestors. In some sense, we have the capacity for creative power akin to that of Olodumare, albeit on a considerably smaller scale. Sacrifice is believed to clear the path, allowing us to gain a clearer understanding of our life's purpose and better manifest our destined achievements.

It is considered the force that amplifies one's Ase and facilitates the realignment of a person's life with their intended path in harmony with their destiny. Babalawos and other initiated individuals, following a divination consultation for themselves, must also do their Ebo. It is important to note that performing Ebo after a reading is something we all do, regardless of being initiated or not. Also, Divination itself is seen as having two main components: first, the reading itself, and second, the Ebo. Here is a look at some of the most common reasons Ebo is done following a reading:

THE PURPOSE AND ROLE OF EBO IN YORUBA SPIRITUAL PRACTICE

• *Ebo is seen as essential for shifting misfortunes into fortunes.*

• *Ebo may be performed for protection and to prevent harm from negative forces or harmful entities.*

• *Ebo may be performed for the purpose of healing and overcoming a difficult illness or life situation that is too overwhelming for the person to handle on their own.*

• *Ebo can help restore balance and harmony in one's life by addressing imbalances or disturbances detected during the divination reading.*

• *Ebo can sometimes be used to help resolve conflicts or disputes within families or communities by seeking divine intervention.*

* * *

It is often believed that refusing to do Ebo after a reading will not help the client and may even cause a worsening of the client's problems. This is a very common belief amongst many Orisha practitioners, and this belief is equally held throughout the Yoruba diaspora. It is said that Ebo is a child of the Orisha Orunmila, meaning that without Ebo, it is believed nothing works. Ebo may be viewed by some practitioners as the oil that greases the parts of the machine of your life and gets rid of the rust so all the components can function properly.

LET US GO THROUGH SOME BASIC INFORMATION
ABOUT EBO AND DIVINATION

Guidance from a Priest or Priestess is crucial when performing any type of Ebo. A non-initiated person should not attempt to perform Ebo on their own without guidance. This can be dangerous and confusing if the non-initiated person does not have the knowledge to do it correctly. Not all Ebo requires blood and the sacrifice of an animal. Ebo can be mainly divided into two different groups: blood sacrifice, which is referred to as *"Ebo Eje"*, and bloodless sacrifice, commonly referred to as an *"Adimu, Adura, Iwa"*.

- **Adimu:** The term "adimu" often translates to "giving thanks" and is frequently used to refer to a food or drink offering prepared for either an Orisha or an ancestor. An adimu can be as simple as offering a glass of water or as complex as preparing a feast. It is often accompanied by Adura, which translates as prayer, devotion, and dedication.
- **Ebo Adura:** "prayer." Sometimes, an Orisha may request the client to be more devotional and dedicated to a particular Orisha or ancestor. This type of sacrifice may take the form of spending time sitting in front of one's shrine for a specific amount of time each week, sitting in nature where a particular Orisha is present for a certain amount of time in meditation or prayer to that Orisha, or ensuring that one's shrine is cleaned more frequently. These are just a few examples of what Adura could consist of.

- **Ebo Iwa:** Iwa means "character." This type of sacrifice often involves changing a person's character or behavior, as sometimes requested by an Orisha.
- **Etutu:** An offering often given to the ancestors, usually in the form of an Adimu.
- **Akose:** A purification, cleansing, or healing mixture of herbs and various items used for healing and purification.

* * *

Please note that an Ebo Eje may or may not be required with an Akose, Ebo Iwa, Ebo Adura, or Adimu, etc. Sometimes, both an Ebo Eje and an Adimu, along with Ebo Adura, are required in a ritual called Eboriru.

- **Eboriru:** Often practiced by Orisha priests, especially Babalawos, it involves prayers (Adura) and may include both Ebo Eje (blood sacrifice) and Adimu (food offerings). This method is viewed as the traditional way of offering Ebo by some Orisha practitioners.
- **Ipese:** means to appease and make things right, sometimes used to refer to an offering given to the *Iyaami*, the mothers.

* * *

Orisha Spirituality and the Controversy of Sacrifice in Western Countries

In Orisha Spirituality, humans are seen as sacred and embody a divine Consciousness, which we call *Ori*. Each person possesses a unique destiny and is considered divine. It is believed that humans have a divine purpose on Earth to assist Olodumare (God) in the continual creation and caring for the physical world we call Earth. Humans are also here to learn how to evolve and grow spiritually.

While animals have a purpose, we believe that they lack certain divine qualities we as humans possess.

The primary purpose of Ifa and Orisha spiritual science is to heal, save, protect, and enhance human life, aiming to provide enlightenment for the betterment of life on Earth. Orisha spirituality focuses on the preservation of life. Orunmila, who came to Earth thousands of years ago, taught divination to humanity to help them save lives. Unfortunately, some individuals interested in demonizing Orisha spirituality approach it with a closed mind, aiming to taunt its followers and instill fear in those with little to no knowledge of the religion. Their goal is often to aggressively convert others to their authoritarian belief systems. This has led to widespread misunderstanding and bias in the public eye. Sadly, there are more people out there attempting to attack us than there are those who support our right to freedom of religion.

We are often described by our critics as "devil worshippers" or "believers in Satan" amongst other things. This has in the past and currently leads to widespread discrimination against us, making us a persecuted minority. Unfortunately, when it comes to persecution, old ways *never* seem to die out, this bias, especially from certain mainstream religious individuals, has led to false claims, such as equating animal sacrifice with human sacrifice, worshipping "Satan" as mentioned above, and numerous other bizarre accusations put on us for simply practicing our right to believe and worship the way we desire peacefully. What these hateful individuals are willing to say about us and every other belief system that they deem unworthy of God's salvation causes us to be stigmatized in the media. Given that we are such a small community, it can be difficult for us to defend ourselves against these vicious attacks. We, as Orisha practitioners, often respect animal and human life more than some other cultures and religions. Just look at the cruelty practiced within the Western slaughterhouses.

The practice of animal sacrifice is deeply rooted in traditional African culture, where it serves as a primary food source. We also have strict regulations on how animal sacrifice is performed and strictly regulate who can and cannot perform it. Below are some guidelines on the subject matter:

1. *The person must have permission from a legitimate priest or priestess and be a legitimate priest or priestess of the tradition themself to be able to perform the animal sacrifice.*
2. *An Orisha or other spiritual entity must deem it as necessary through means of divination, and the individual must be properly trained to be able to perform it.*
3. *Animal sacrifice requires training and various instructions from a legitimate priest or priestess of the tradition and should not be performed by an inexperienced or uninitiated individual. Taking the life of an animal is a serious act and should not be taken lightly.*

* * *

My Emergency Item List

I often keep the following items on hand just in case I need to do a divination and make a quick offering. I suggest the following:

A small white candle: Used to bring light, illumination, and clarity. One can also read the flame to determine what spiritual energies are around the individual. Candles can be helpful in determining how the Orisha feels, whether the Orisha is content or not.

Common Food Offerings to Keep on Hand

- **Coconut:** *Sometimes a whole coconut is given, other times only coconut oil or coconut water.*

- **Rum or gin:** *Often a needed item for some of the warrior male Orishas.*
- **Palm oil:** *Often, Eshu and Orunmila will ask for palm oil.*
- **Incense sticks:** *Oya may ask for an offering of incense.*
- **Water:** *The first thing to ask. Water is given as an offering to all the deities and is used to cleanse and purify.*
- **Honey:** *Used to make things sweet, given as an offering to bring forth sweetness in life.*
- **Flowers:** *Given to all the Orishas, particularly to the ancestors, as a symbol of health and happiness.*
- **Effun or Cascarilla:** *This item is seen as sacred to the Orisha Obatala and can be used to cleanse space or mark sacred space by drawing a circle with it and putting offerings in the circle.*
- **Candies:** *Sometimes we give candies to the Orisha Eshu/Elegua.*
- **Corn flour:** *This is used to make what is called "eko." It is cornmeal made from corn flour and water. This is given as a common food offering to many of the Orishas.*
- **Fruits:** *Representing abundance, vitality, and nourishment, they are occasionally offered to bring sweetness into life.*

In conclusion, sacrifice, known as "Ebo," holds significant importance in the Orisha tradition. It serves to connect with the spiritual world, transform misfortunes into fortunes, and seek protection, healing, and balance in one's life. Ebo is a fundamental aspect of divination and essential for those seeking guidance and assistance from the Orishas.

It's important to approach Ebo with guidance from a Priest or Priestess, recognizing that not all Ebo requires blood sacrifice. While animal sacrifice is a part of this religion, it is not always mandatory. Understanding the cultural significance and context of these practices within the broader religious landscape is crucial, especially in non-Western belief systems that may have different standards. Within Orisha spirituality, the preservation of human life is central to our religion. A Babalawo will not hesitate to sacrifice an animal if it is required to save a human life.

* * *

CHAPTER 17

IRE AND IBI: EMBRACING DESTINY'S BALANCE

IN THIS CHAPTER, we explore the spiritual energies known as Ire (blessings) and Ibi (challenges). The Yoruba believe that each person enters the world with a predetermined destiny and can either align with it or stray from it. This alignment is referred to as "Ire" or "Ibi," sometimes replaced with "Osogbo" in the diaspora. When in "Ire," life is in balance with one's destiny, bringing blessings and good things. Conversely, when one is out of alignment, despite efforts, it's believed they are in "Ibi" or experiencing challenges. Problems within Ire are usually less severe, but when they intensify, it's advised to consult a Babalawo or priest to determine if one is in Osogbo, Ibi, or Ayewo, indicating misalignment with destiny and blessings.

The term "*Ibi*" is often misunderstood due to its lost meaning in translation. "*Ibi*" means the thing that challenges or questions a person. The common translation often portrays "*Ibi*" as bad or wrong, but this is incorrect. "Ibi" often signifies the force that prompts us to question challenging situations in our lives. It frequently manifests as misfortune that is difficult or hard to accept, leading us to ask ourselves, "Why is this happening to me?" Orisha practitioners may attribute misfortune to a spirit called Elenini, believed to deliver Ibi or Osogbo. Some regard Elenini as a demon, while others see it as a negative aspect of our spiritual consciousness that impedes spiritual growth. Failure to address life's imbalances can lead Elenini to manifest in various ways, often when we engage in poor moral judgment or inappropriate activities. Overcoming Elenini and Ibi often demands good character, sacrifice, and patience. Ebo, an offering, helps ward off Ibi and attract Ire. Everyone is believed to enter the world with a unique purpose or destiny. Straying from one's own destiny and following another can disrupt alignment. Divination seeks guidance from divinities on necessary changes to realign with our destiny. Being in alignment, or "being in Ire," signifies balance and harmony with one's destiny. Even on our chosen path, Osogbo may still manifest, emphasizing the importance of readings and Ebo. Ebo serves to repel Ibi and attract Ire. Ire and Ibi, sometimes called, Osogbo or Ayewo function as guiding principles, fostering spiritual growth and life balance. Ibi presents opportunities for learning and growth, while Ire brings the sweetness of life. Ebo plays a protective role in this process.

* * *

In the following story found in the Odu: **Okanran Meji**, we can gain insight into the relationship between Ire (blessings) and Ibi (to question misfortune). This tale is known as **"The Divine Rivalry"** between two brothers:

Once upon a time, there were two brothers. One was named "The One Who Brings Blessings," and the other "The One Who Brings Misfortune." Both were great warriors but as different as day and night, constantly competing to prove their superiority. Over time, their ongoing strife disturbed many divinities. As days turned into nights, the brothers' resentment grew. One day, Olorun, the Lord of the Heavens, overheard their quarrels and decided to end the conflict. He summoned the brothers and asked why they fought. They both replied that they wanted to know who possessed the greatest amount of Ase (spiritual power). Olorun commanded both to perform a sacrifice (ebó) and appear before him the next morning. The elder brother, "The One Who Brings Blessings," believed he had plenty of time and decided to delay the sacrifice until morning. Meanwhile, "The One Who Brings Misfortune," the younger brother, immediately prepared and performed the sacrifice that evening. The next morning, "The One Who Brings Blessings" overslept and arrived late at Olorun's house, while "The One Who Brings Misfortune" was already there. When Olorun asked if they had obeyed his instructions, "The One Who Brings Blessings" admitted he had not completed the ebó in time. "The One Who Brings Misfortune" proudly declared he had followed all the instructions.

Pleased with the younger brother's obedience, Olorun decreed that "Misfortune" would have dominion over the world. He also declared that "The One Who Brings Blessings" would only exist in one place at a time and appear briefly, while "Misfortune" could appear in multiple places simultaneously. This story teaches that Ire (blessings) became known as the spirit of unreliability, while Ibi (misfortune) became the spirit of reliability. Misfortune rules the world, while blessings manifest briefly in one's life. When blessings do appear, we must seize the opportunity, as they are rare and fleeting.

A LIST OF DIFFERENT TYPES OF IRE AND IBI

In life, blessings and misfortune can manifest in various forms. Below is a list of some of the different types of Ire and Ibi or Osogbo:

Various Osogbos and Ibís (Misfortunes) that can manifest in our lives:

- **Osogbo Ikú:** *Death.*
- **Osogbo Ofo:** *Loss and grief.*
- **Osogbo Arun:** *Disease and sickness.*

- **Osogbo Ewon:** *Imprisonment and loss of freedom.*
- **Osogbo Ina:** *War, arguments, envy, and gossip.*
- **Osogbo Oran:** *Trouble and crime.*
- **Osogbo Ogu:** *Curses through witchcraft.*
- **Osogbo Ona:** *Struggles currently or ahead.*

Various Irès (Blessings) that can manifest in our lives:

- **Ire Abilona:** *Open roads ahead.*
- **Ire Didara:** *Wellness.*
- **Ire Aje:** *Wealth.*
- **Ire Aiku:** *Health, longevity, life.*
- **Ire Lalafia:** *Happiness.*
- **Ire Omo:** *Children.*
- **Ire Owo:** *Money.*
- **Ire Loshowo:** *Blessings through commerce and business.*

In the delicate balance of Ire and Ibi, we find the essence of life's journey. By aligning with our destiny and embracing divination and rituals, we navigate challenges with resilience and invite the blessings of Ire. Misfortune, often a disguised teacher, offers lessons that shape our spiritual growth and help us recognise when we are out of alignment with fate. Through these intertwined forces, we learn and spiritually evolve.

* * *

CHAPTER 18

INTRODUCTION TO OBI DIVINATION

WELCOME to the mystical realm of Obi divination, a sacred practice deeply rooted in the ancient Yoruba spiritual tradition and embraced by Yoruba people and their descendants around the world. Obi is the cornerstone and foundation of the Yoruba divination system. While it serves as the starting point, this system is far from simple, offering many layers to explore. In this chapter, we will examine the five basic combinations. In the next chapter, we will delve into the more advanced aspects of this ancient system. We will begin our study of Obi divination with an introduction to the story of the Orisha Obi, found in the Odu **Obara-Osa**. This story has multiple versions, and the one below is the version I was told:

THE STORY OF THE ORISHA OBI

In the ancient days, when both the Orishas and humans inhabited the world, and the portal between the heavens and the earth was not yet closed, there was an Orisha named Obi. He served and praised Olofin with such beauty and grace that Olofin blessed him with immense strength, wisdom, and Ase. Olofin saw great potential in Obi and gave him a task to go out into the world and serve humans as a diviner, helping them find their way. Obi quickly became famous for his ability to heal and help those who came to him. Many people sought Obi's guidance.

However, over time, Obi became prideful and arrogant, seeing how much the humans depended on his guidance. He started demanding a lot of cowries (money) for his services and pushed away people who couldn't afford to pay, showing disdain for the less fortunate.

One day, Eshu, a friend of Obi, heard about Obi's arrogance and decided to see if the rumors were in fact true. Disguised as a beggar, Eshu went to Obi's house and asked for help, offering only a Coconut in return. To Eshu's surprise, Obi cursed him and chased him away, forbidding him to return.

Disturbed by Obi's behavior, Eshu went to Olofin and told God what had happened. Olofin decided to also disguise himself as a beggar and ask Obi for help. When Obi opened the door, he became furious seeing a beggar standing before him. At that point, Olofin revealed his true identity to Obi, and once Obi realized what he had done, he fell to his knees begging for forgiveness. Olofin, saddened by Obi's transformation from a pure and respected Orisha to an arrogant being, took away Obi's voice and outer beauty, turning him into a Coconut. Olofin punished Obi by hanging him high in the tree to symbolize his arrogance, but he will never stay there permanently, for once he falls, he will hit the ground.

It is also said that Olofin kept Obi pure and white inside and made his outer shell ugly and brown so people can remember Obi's purity and devotion to Olofin before he was tainted with ugliness and greed.

The story continues, from that day forward, Obi could only speak when permitted by others, as a punishment for his pride. Olofin instructed Obi to serve all who came to him sincerely and truthfully, regardless of their status or position. Obi became a servant to all who sought his help, his power now manifested through the Coconut. Obi's punishment served as a reminder that true character is measured not by one's strength or status *but by their kindness and respect towards others, especially those less fortunate.*

* * *

This story teaches us that true beauty lies not in outward appearances, but in our inward character. It also serves as a warning that we must always strive to have a gentle character, or iwa pele. Obi's arrogance led to his downfall, demonstrating the dangers of having a bad character. His transformation serves as a poignant metaphor for the potential within each of us to rise above our ego and embrace **Omoluwabi**, which is the Yoruba ideal of someone who strives to have good character in life.

Obi is an Orisha, and you should always approach him with respect like any other Orisha in the Yoruba pantheon. Obi divination is also seen as a sacred connection between the Orisha and the participants within the Orisha Spirituality. *Advice: I suggest to my readers that they use caution if they decide to mix traditional Yoruba, Orisha practices with any outside non-Yoruba tradition, culture, or practice. Always ask permission of the Orishas or any other spirits if it is permissible prior to doing this.*

THE HISTORY OF OBI DIVINATION

We seek advice from *OBI* for various reasons, including guidance for crucial life choices, help in resolving dilemmas, gaining insight into the present and future, connecting with ancestors and spiritual guides, and receiving healing and guidance for oneself and others. OBI divination is a valuable tool for anyone seeking direction on their life path. It assists in making wise decisions, overcoming challenges, and connecting with our spiritual selves. There are two types of Obi divination: *Obi Abata and Obi Agbon.* The main difference lies in the particular type of nut that is used for divination. Obi Abata uses the four-lobed nut from the Kola plant (*Cola acuminata*), while

Obi Agbon uses the coconut from the Cocos nucifera tree as a substitute. *Obi Abata* is considered the oldest form of Obi and is more traditional. It is still used in Africa today.

During the Atlantic Slave Trade, Africans learned to substitute the Kola nut with the coconut, which was more accessible in the New World. This is when Obi began being associated with the coconut from the Cocos nucifera tree. *Obi Agbon* divination is simpler to learn than the traditional Obi Abata and is more prevalent and common today, especially in the Americas, Caribbean, and amongst traditions like Santeria and Candomblé, both practiced in Cuba and Brazil. Traditional *Obi Abata* is sometimes used by various communities and practitioners in North America, but the Kola often needs to be imported from Africa. The choice between *Obi Abata* and Obi Agbon depends on tradition and local practices, emphasizing lineage and regional traditions within Orisha spirituality. Both Obi Abata and *Obi Agbon* are valid, reflecting the diversity of Yoruba spiritual practices.

This chapter will focus on *Obi Agbon* divination because it is the simplest and easiest form of Obi to learn. *Obi Agbon* makes five main patterns: **Alafia, Ejife, Etawa, Okanran,** and **Oyeku.** These five patterns are determined by the way the coconut pieces drop on the ground when the diviner holds them in their hands and drops them onto a mat or the floor. Regardless of how you drop the four pieces of coconut, they can only land in five combinations. It is sometimes common to use four cowrie shells in place of four pieces of coconut shell. We will be discussing how to interpret both the shells and the coconuts within this chapter.

In every divination system in the Yoruba tradition, the patterns formed during divination are referred to as **Odus**. Again, the main Odus of Obi are **Alafia, Ejife, Etawa, Okanran,** *and* **Oyeku**. In Obi Abata, these same Odus are used, along with several additional ones. We will discuss Obi Abata further in the next chapter. In both Obi

Abata and Obi Agbon, the diviner interprets the patterns based on their knowledge of Yoruba tradition and the individual's situation.

Each pattern holds a unique meaning, which the diviner uses to offer guidance and support. Obi divination is a powerful tool for gaining insights into one's life and path. This tradition has been passed down for generations.

* * *

UNDERSTANDING THE COCONUT

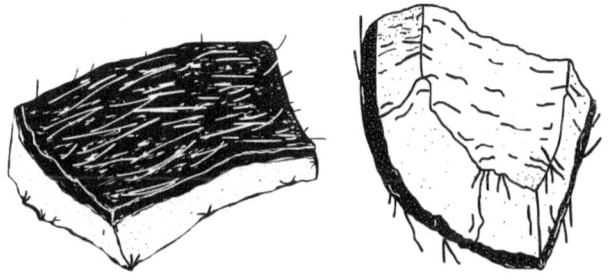

In the image above, there are two pieces of coconut shell. On the left side, the dark piece, commonly called the coconut shell, is facing upward, while on the right side, the white part of the coconut, known as the coconut meat, is also facing upward. Alternatively, the piece on the left has the meat of the coconut facing downward. In Obi divination, a coconut piece with the meat facing downward is in the "closed" position, meaning this piece is not speaking. The piece on the right, with the meat facing upward, is in the "open" position, meaning it is speaking. We can represent these two pieces by the letters X and O, where O symbolizes the open piece, and X symbolizes the closed piece. This would make the pattern XO.

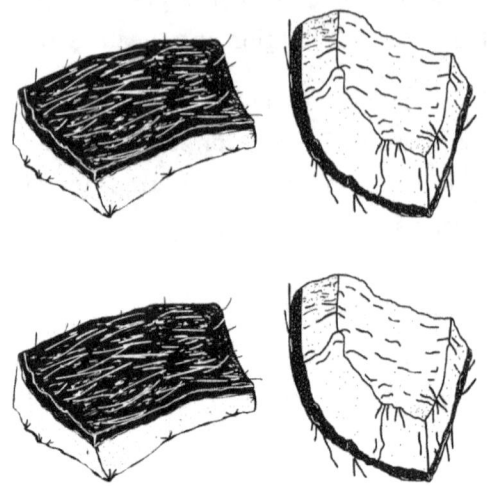

The pattern called Ejife is formed by four coconut pieces as seen in the image above: two open and two closed. Using X and O, where X represents a closed piece, and O represents an open piece, Ejife would be represented as "XX" on the left and "OO" on the right, forming the pattern "XXOO." Ejife generally signifies balance in whatever was asked during the Obi consultation. It means that the energies in a situation are in balance, and no further offerings or ebos are needed. Ejife is considered one of the most positive outcomes in an Obi divination.

HOW TO DIVINE WITH
COWRIE SHELLS

CLOSED/ NOT SPEAKING

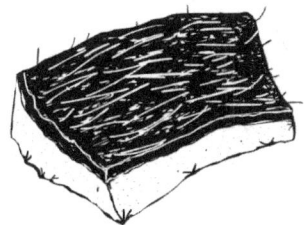 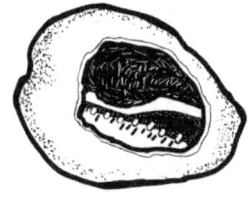

OPEN/ SPEAKING

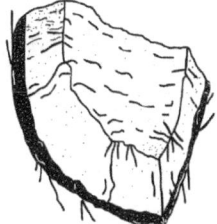 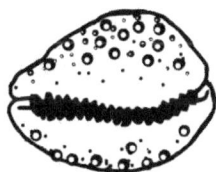

As you can see in the image above, the cowrie shell and the coconut piece at the top are in closed positions, making the pattern "XX." At the bottom, both the cowrie shell and the coconut piece are in open positions, making the pattern "OO." The entire image forms the pattern Ejife, using both cowrie shells and coconut pieces. This demonstrates how you can substitute cowrie shells for coconut pieces and or coconut pieces for cowrie shells when performing divination.

* * *

READING THE OBI PATTERNS

Below is a list and description of the Obi patterns using cowrie shells to represent the patterns: **Ejife, Alafia, Etawa, Okanran,** and **Oyeku.**

THE PATTERN EJIFE

<u>Ejife</u>: The image below shows the Obi Odu pattern of Ejife "OOXX". There are two male shells closed on top, facing downwards, that do not bring light to the situation, and two female shells open on the bottom, facing upwards, that bring light.

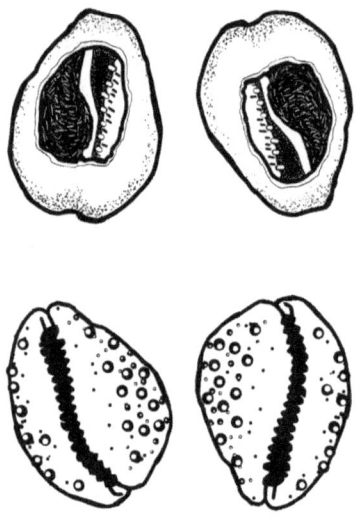

INTERPRETATIONS OF EJIFE

A balance between the forces of light and darkness or between blessings and obstacles on the journey, the importance of making balanced decisions, weighing the good and the bad before moving forward. When asking yes or no questions, Ejife often means "yes" but to proceed with balanced judgment. This pattern indicates that life is not direct and that there will be challenges and blessings on our way. This pattern also talks about being grounded or the importance of being grounded. The blessings are seen as the female shells on the bottom facing up and open. The Odu- Ejife is often seen as coming in IRE and is more positive than negative. ***Orishas and divinities associated with this sign are the Ibejis, Oshun, Obatala, Eshu/Elegua, Yemoja, Oshunmare, Ochosi, and Ori.***

* * *

THE PATTERN ALAFIA.

Alafia: This image below shows the pattern Alafia. There are four female shells all facing upwards and are open, creating the pattern "OOOO"

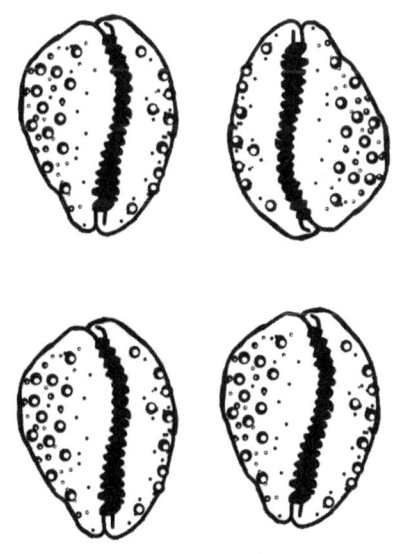

INTERPRETATIONS OF ALAFIA

When this pattern appears, we believe there is no need to re-ask the question again. Alafia often means a certain "yes". This pattern radiates with pure light and there is no darkness here within. This sign is often interpreted as being clear, having clarity in a situation, that all energies in a situation are positively flowing in the direction of ire. Alafia is the most positive sign in Obi. This sign is seen as a symbol of peace and blessing and is sometimes used by Orisha practitioners as a greeting rather than saying "hello". The sign of Alafia comes in Ire. One caution with this sign is that this energy can be overwhelming, and it can present itself to us all at once. Make sure to maintain balance in moving forward. ***Orishas and divinities associated with this sign are Obatala, Olodumare, Orunmila / IFA, Shango, Oshunmare and Ori.***

Etawa: The image below shows the Etawa pattern. There are three shells open and one closed. Creating the pattern "OOOX"

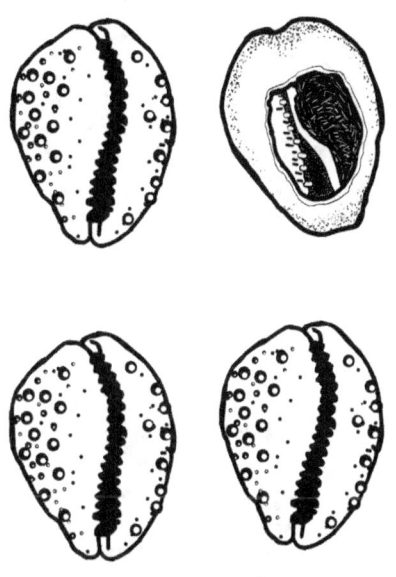

INTERPRETATIONS OF ETAWA

When asking a yes or no question Etawa is seen as a "maybe or a yes but something is missing and is absent." The one shell in the right corner is not facing in the same direction as the other shells and this shell is considered closed. This energy pattern is seen as being imbalanced and not complete. There is light in this situation than darkness, but something is still missing. One question that is often asked following this combination is for the need of sacrifice. I like to say that Etawa is an incomplete Alafia. Some When Etawa appears this Odu still comes in IRE because there is still more light than darkness. **Orishas and other divinities associated with this sign include Shango, Ogun, Eshu/ Eleggua, and Yemonja.**

Okanran: The image below shows the Okanran pattern. Creating the pattern: "OXXX"

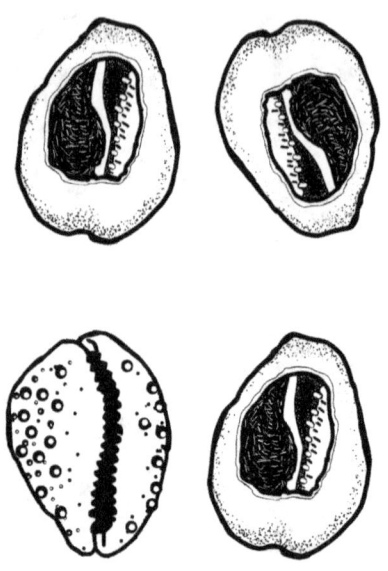

INTERPRETATIONS OF OKANRAN

This energy pattern is made up of more darkness than light. This sign often indicates the following: difficulty, a struggle, much confusion in a situation, many roadblocks and obstacles, limited light, unable to see very far ahead or forward. When asking yes or no questions, okanran often indicates a "no." This sign may also be interpreted as some that is draining a person's energy or resources. Sometimes it may be necessary to seek the help of the Orishas or ancestors to be victorious when Okanran appears. One question that is often asked following this combination is for the need of Ebo or sacrifices to turn this sign into ire. When Okanran appears, this Odu rarely comes in IRE. ***Orishas and other spiritual forces associated*** *with this Odu are Chango, Osain, Ogun, and Babalu-aye, and Aganju.*

* * *

Oyeku: The image below shows the Oyeku pattern. In this pattern, all shells are closed and facing downward. Creating the pattern: "XXXX"

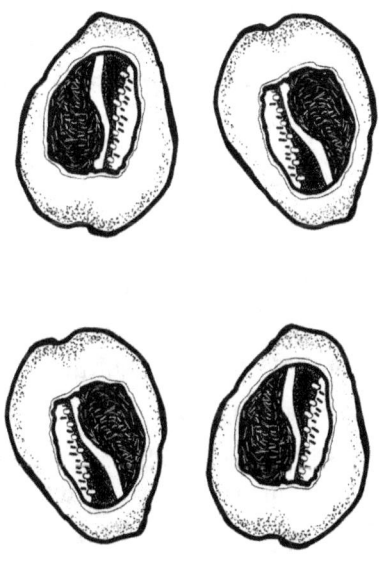

INTERPRETATIONS OF OYEKU

When this pattern appears we often seek the assistance of the spirits for help and guidance. This energy matrix indicates a total and complete lack of light and total darkness. Some interpretations may include total and complete darkness, nothing good can come from the darkness, negative energy surrounding a situation where there are no blessings, being out of alignment with destiny, the need for an ori cleansing and possibly the need to do Ebo, not being able to find or see a way out. When asking a yes or no question and Oyeku appears we often interpret this energy matrix as an absolute "no" Oyeku can indicate that the dead or the ancestors are trying to help the person find a way out of a situation. Other meanings include A time for renewal, a time to pursue a new direction and a time to throw things away and start fresh. When someone receives this pattern, the following questions are often asked: Are the ancestors asking for an offering? Does my Ori need to be fed or washed? Does any other orisha need to be fed? If the question was about a circumstance, when receiving this pattern, one should not ask again. *Orishas and other spiritual forces associated with this Odu are Ancestors and the Dead, Orisha Egungun, Oya, Babalu-aye, Yewa, Olokun, Ogun and Iku.*

* * *

HOW TO ASK QUESTIONS

When performing divination and consulting either the Orishas or any other spirit, we need to pay close attention to how we formulate and ask questions. Most often, the answers are determined by how we asked the questions. This is why we need to be careful to formulate our questions before asking them. Here are some tips for asking in the correct way.

1. **Avoid Vague Questions**: First and foremost, one should avoid being too vague. Being vague may give rise to multiple interpretations of the question, and for this reason, vaguely defined questions should be avoided. Avoid asking questions with the words "could" or "can."

2. **Be Precise**: Why are you asking the question? Instead of asking the question, "Should I take that new job, or should I move to that new city?" ask, put in front of that question, "Is it in my

194

highest purpose, and does it align with my destiny, to take this new job?"

3. **Avoid Repetition:** Refrain from posing the same question more than once unless the question was badly formulated.

4. **Avoid Deception:** If you already know something to be true, do not ask the question. In this situation, the Orishas or your own Ori could intentionally mislead you, knowing that you know the answer to the question already. It is best to avoid asking questions if you already know the answers to them.

It is important to respect the answers given during the cast when questions are asked correctly. However, you may reframe and ask the same question differently if the original answer was vague. For example, "Should I move to California?" is vaguer than "Is it my highest purpose and aligned with my destiny to move to California?" If the original question lacked a timeframe, you can ask again with a specified period. For instance, the question "Is it my highest purpose and aligned with my destiny to move to California?" has no time-frame. You could rephrase it to "Is it in my highest purpose and aligned with my destiny to move to California at this time?" or "Is it my highest purpose and aligned with my destiny to move to California in the next six months?"

In these cases, it is acceptable to ask again. However, if you receive a "No" to the question, you should typically refrain from asking the same question again until the specified timeframe has passed.

WHEN NEEDING TO ASK MORE
THAN ONE QUESTION

Sometimes you may decide to ask a second time. If you receive Ejife, Alafia, or Oyeku, you often don't need to ask the same question again. However, if you receive Okanran or Etawa, you may need to throw or ask again. Below are the combinations when re-asking.

Note: When you throw either an Alafia or an Ejife, they both signify a "yes" and there is no need to throw again. If you receive also an Oyeku we often need to ask if the ancestors need something or the Orishas and often times we will also wait a few days before asking a similar again using Obi.

INTERPRETATIONS OF OTHER COMBINATIONS

- **Okanran + Alafia**: Yes, but be careful not to be overwhelmed when blessings all come at once.
- **Okanran + Ejife**: Yes, balance can be achieved; however, it is important to work hard to maintain it.
- **Okanran + Okanran**: Unlikely. This combination indicates a significant imbalance, and without significant hard work, the odds of achieving balance are slim.
- **Okanran + Etawa**: Maybe. This combination suggests that something is either missing, still out of balance, or a key issue is not being considered.
- **Okanran + Oyeku**: No. It is best to pursue other options as this combination indicates that the situation might be out of our hands.
- **Etawa + Alafia**: Likely, but be careful not to be overwhelmed when blessings all come at once.
- **Etawa + Ejife**: Yes, for now. However, it is important to consider something that may have been overlooked to maintain this balance.
- **Etawa + Okanran**: No. A significant imbalance exists, and without substantial effort, achieving balance is unlikely.
- **Etawa + Etawa**: Maybe. This combination indicates that something is either missing, still out of balance, or a key issue is not being considered.
- **Etawa + Oyeku**: No. This combination often indicates that achieving balance in the situation will be very difficult, even with hard work.

When asking questions in divination, it is important to be clear, concise, and respectful. Avoid asking vague, repetitive, or deceptive questions. If you receive a vague answer, you may reframe the question and ask again. However, if you receive a "No," it is best to refrain from asking the same question again until the time frame has passed.

It is also important to keep a record of your readings and questions in a notebook with the dates and the answers as well as the Odus you received so that you can track your progress, learn from your experiences, and keep record of clients you have worked with. During a divination session it is important to do the following:

- *Be open to receiving unexpected answers.*
- *Be respectful of the answers you receive, even if you don't like them.*
- *Use your intuition to interpret the answers you receive.*
- *Trust that you are receiving the information you need, even if you don't understand it fully.*

Remember, Orishas and spirits are their own entities, and they often give unexpected responses. This is because they have a different perspective on our lives than we do. They can see things that we cannot, and they may give us answers that we do not want to hear nor understand, and this is why it is important for the diviner to be properly informed and trained and initiated before taking upon themselves the process of engaging in any interaction with a spirit, especially a spirit or divinity they have not worked with prior.

HOW TO MAKE YOUR OWN OBI SET

For Obi Agbon divination, you have several options for constructing your own set. You can use 4 cowrie shells, with or without the backs sanded off, as shown in the photos above. Alternatively, you can use four pieces of coconut shell that have been sanded down and polished, or opt for a fresh coconut. If using a fresh coconut or fresh kola nuts, there's no need to bless the Obi separately, as their natural state already carries the blessing.

* * *

STEP 1.
Acquire at least four small coconut shells that are small enough to hold in one hand from a fresh coconut. Clean them thoroughly pulling off the white meat and sand them using either sandpaper or a sander. Note: It is important when breaking the coconut not to slam the coconut to the ground, this can be considered disrespectful to Obi.

STEP 2
Paint the inner side of the shells with white paint where the coconut meat was originally.

STEP 3.
Polish your Obi shells with a rag and some coconut oil. Adding a drop of lavender essential oil to the coconut oil helps expel any negative energies. The coconut oil also serves to both feed your Obi shells and make them water-resistant. It's a good practice to rub coconut oil on your Obi before each use.

STEP 4.
Next, you'll need some alcohol, preferably rum or gin, and honey.

The honey is used to bring sweetness and blessings (Ire), counteracting any negative aspects (Osogbo).

STEP 5.
Mix a little honey into your spirits. After rubbing coconut oil on your Obi, take a small amount of this mixture into your mouth and blow it lightly onto the Obi.

STEP 6.
Light a candle to represent the light and clarity you seek in your life. If outdoors during the daytime, you can skip this step. It is important to still say the candle lighting prayer below in this step.

STEP 7.
Prepare a glass of water to purify the space before casting Obi. You can use a white cloth, a grass mat, or a white handkerchief as a surface for casting Obi. The handkerchief can also serve as a storage place for your Obi.

STEP 8.
Recite the prayers to ensure your Obi is ready for divination.

* * *

THE PRAYERS FOR INVOKING OBI

When lighting the candle in step 6, recite the following prayers below:

Divine Creator of all things, we come before you to honor the sacred flame that gives light and wisdom. We acknowledge the power and beauty of this flame, which illuminates our path and guides us towards the truth. We ask that you bless this flame with your presence and your love, and that you help us to receive its wisdom and teachings. May this flame inspire us to seek knowledge and understanding, and may it help us to grow in wisdom and compassion. May this sacred flame also provide us with the light we need to navigate the challenges and obstacles of our lives. May it give us the clarity and courage to face our fears and overcome our limitations.

Now, we will recite the Omi Tutu prayer.

First, as mentioned above, Obtain a small bowl of water.

Dab your finger in the water and let it drop on the **GROUND,** then recite the verses below:

Omi Tutu, Omi Tutu: Cool water, fresh Water
Omi Tutu, Omi Tutu: Cool water, fresh Water
Omi Tutu, Omi Tutu: Cool water, fresh Water

Again, dab your finger in the water and let it drop on the **GROUND,** then recite the verse below:

Omi Tutu: Cool water, fresh Water
Ile Tutu: Refresh the house

Again, dab your finger in the water and let it drop on the **GROUND,** then recite the verse below:

Omi Tutu: Cool water, fresh Water
Ona Tutu: Refresh my roads

Again, dab your finger in the water and let it drop on the **GROUND,** then recite the verse below:

Omi Tutu: Cool water fresh Water
Egun Tutu: Refresh the ancestors

Again, dab your finger in the water and let it drop on the top of your **HEAD,** then recite the verse below:

Omi Tutu: Cool water, fresh Water
Ori Tutu: Refresh and cool my Ori

Again, dab your finger in the water and let it drop on the **GROUND** then recite the verse below:

Tutu Eshu: Refresh Eshu, the messenger
Tutu Orishas: Refresh the Orishas

Again, dab your finger in the water and let it drop on the **OBI** pieces, then recite the verse below:

Tutu Obi: Refresh and cool Obi

Again, dab your finger in the water and let it drop on the GROUND then recite the verse below:

Ibase Olodumare: I call upon and praise the creator

ASE, ASE, ASE, Oh...

We will now recite the prayer to obi to invoke obi....

THE OBI PRAYER

Obi ni ibi Iku
Obi averts death.

Obi ni ibi Arun
Obi averts sickness.

Obi ni ibi Ofo
Obi averts loss.

Raise the Obi above your head and say:
May Obi protect me from sudden loss, sudden harm, sudden death, and sudden illness. May Obi be imbued with the Ase of Olodumare so that Obi can reveal the answers that I seek in truth and in clarity.

Ibase Olodumare: I call upon and praise the creator

Ashe, Ashe, Ashe, Ooh...
✱✱

Hold your OBI in both hands, blow on them with your breath, ask OBI your question, and then cast the OBI

Diviners often cast Obi on a flat surface; any surface will work however, for a more traditional practice, a Babalawo will often cast obi either on a grass mat or a diviner's tray called an Opon IFA. I have also seen Obi cast on white or leather cloth as well.

How should I store my obi?

Obi, being a sacred tool, requires respectful handling. It is advisable to keep obi tied up in a cloth, bag, or small container. All obi tools should be stored together in one designated place. Some individuals prefer to store obi near Orisha shrines, while others dedicate their obi to a specific Orisha. Dedicated obi should be kept near the Orisha or Ancestor altars they are dedicated to, as they become the possession of the Orisha or the ancestors and should be stored near them.

✱ ✱ ✱

CHAPTER 19

OBI ΛBATA DIVINATION

THE BASICS OF OBI ABATA

IN THE LAST CHAPTER, we discussed Obi divination with the coconut, known as Obi Agbon. In this chapter, we will delve further into the Obi Abata divination system, which is said to be over six thousand years old. Obi Abata uses the kola nut for divination rather than the coconut but it functions in many similar ways. Scholars believe that the use of the coconut for Obi Agbon evolved out of necessity due to the scarcity of the kola nut in the New World, particularly in the Caribbean and the Americas. Enslaved people made every effort to preserve this ancient divination form by substituting the coconut for the kola nut.

Unfortunately, in doing so, many of the traditional nine patterns were lost and simplified into the five patterns we discussed in the prior chapter. Obi Abata uses the four-lobed kola nut from the plant Cola acuminata. While there are several different varieties of kola nuts, only the four-lobed kola can be used for divination. Three, two, or one-lobed kola nuts are not used for divination but can serve as offerings and medicine.

Important advice: Do not confuse the bitter kola nut (scientific name: Garcinia kola) with Cola acuminata. While bitter kola is given to various Orishas, it is not used in Obi divination and does not have four segments.

THE STEPS FOR USING OBI ABATA

The first step is to break the Kola nut into four separate sections or segments and then repeat steps 6, 7, and 8 as discussed in the prior chapter and below:

STEP 6
Light a candle to represent the light and clarity you seek in your life. If outdoors during the daytime, you can skip this step. It is important to still say the candle lighting prayer in this step.

STEP 7.
Prepare a glass of water to purify the space before casting Obi. You can use a white cloth, a grass mat, or a white handkerchief as a surface for casting Obi. The handkerchief can also serve as a storage place for your Obi.

STEP 8
Recite the prayers to ensure your Obi is ready for divination.

* * *

THE PRAYERS FOR INVOKING OBI

When lighting the candle in step 6, recite the following prayers below:

Divine Creator of all things, we come before you to honor the sacred flame that gives light and wisdom. We acknowledge the power and beauty of this flame, which illuminates our path and guides us towards the truth. We ask that you bless this flame with your presence and your love, and that you help us to receive its wisdom and teachings. May this flame inspire us to seek knowledge and understanding, and may it help us to grow in wisdom and compassion. May this sacred flame also provide us with the light we need to navigate the challenges and obstacles of our lives. May it give us the clarity and courage to face our fears and overcome our limitations.

The Omi Tutu Prayer

We will now recite the Omi Tutu prayer. Note: Please have a small bowl of water ready for this prayer.

Dab your finger in the water and let it drop on the **GROUND,** then recite the verses below:

Omi Tutu, Omi Tutu: Cool water, fresh Water
Omi Tutu, Omi Tutu: Cool water, fresh Water
Omi Tutu, Omi Tutu: Cool water, fresh Water

Again, dab your finger in the water and let it drop on the **GROUND,** then recite the verse below:

Omi Tutu: Cool water, fresh Water
Ile Tutu: Refresh the house

Again, dab your finger in the water and let it drop on the **GROUND,** then recite the verse below:

Omi Tutu: Cool water ,fresh Water
Ona Tutu: Refresh my roads

Again, dab your finger in the water and let it drop on the **GROUND,** then recite the verse below:

Omi Tutu: Cool water, fresh Water
Egun Tutu: Refresh the ancestors

Again, dab your finger in the water and let it drop on the top of your
HEAD, then recite the verse below:

Omi Tutu: Cool water, fresh Water
Ori Tutu: Refresh and cool my Ori

Again, dab your finger in the water and let it drop on the **GROUND,**
then recite the verse below:

Tutu Eshu: Refresh Eshu, the messenger
Tutu Orishas: Refresh, the Orishas

Again, dab your finger in the water and let it drop on the **OBI,** pieces
then recite the verse below:

Tutu Obi: Refresh and cool Obi

Again, dab your finger in the water and let it drop on the **GROUND,**
then recite the verse below:

Ibase Olodumare: I call upon and praise the creator

ASE, ASE, ASE, Oh...
We will now recite the prayer to obi to invoke obi....

THE OBI PRAYER
Now, we are going to recite the Obi Prayer...

Obi ni ibi Iku
Obi averts death.

Obi ni ibi Arun

Obi averts sickness.

Obi ni ibi Ofo

Obi averts loss.

Raise the Obi above your head and say:

May Obi protect me from sudden loss, sudden harm, sudden death, sudden illness. May Obi be imbued with the Ase of Olodumare so that Obi can reveal the answers that I seek in truth and in clarity.

Ibase Olodumare: I call upon and praise the creator

Ashe, Ashe, Ashe, Ooh...
**

Hold your OBI in both hands, blow on it with your breath, ask OBI your question, and then cast the OBI

Now you can begin to cast...

* * *

Once the Kola nut is divided into four lobes in the first step, as discussed above it will often appear like in the images below.

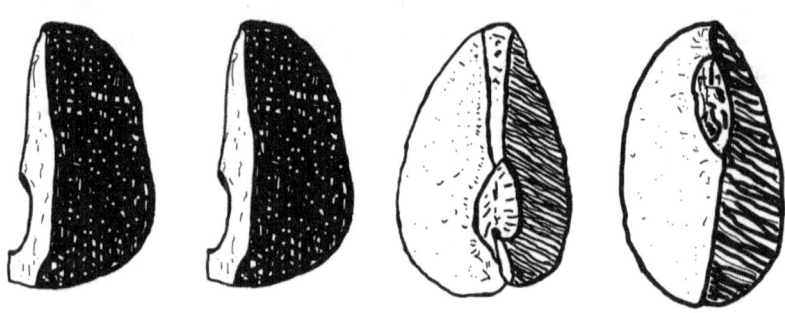

You can see within the image that there are four sections divided with two dark sections on the left facing downward and on the right two pieces facing upwards, the name for this pattern is **Ejife** (please read the prior chapter on the interpretation of Ejife for further information.

OPEN SEGMENTS /
SPEAKING BELOW

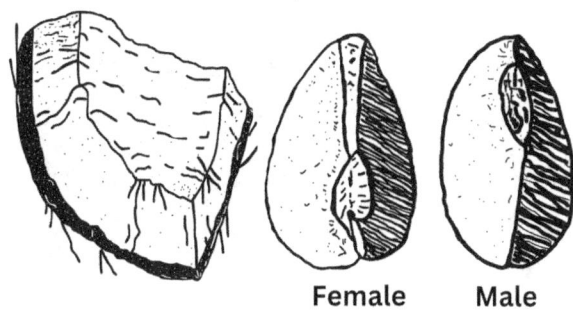

Female   Male

CLOSED SEGMENTS /
NOT SPEAKING BELOW

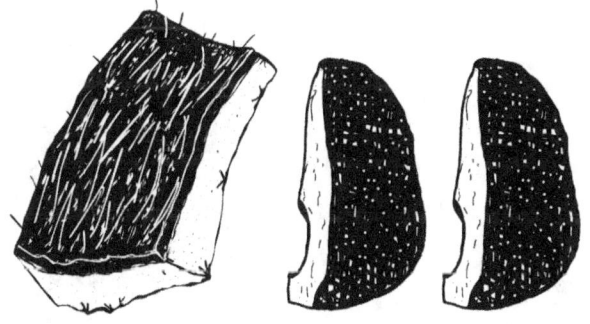

Above you can see that the coconut pieces on the left are facing upwards (open) and downwards (closed) as discussed previously. You can also see on the right side of the coconut pieces the open and closed patterns of the Kola nut. Below you can see this with the cowrie shell as well.

* * *

CLOSED SEGMENTS/
NOT SPEAKING BELOW

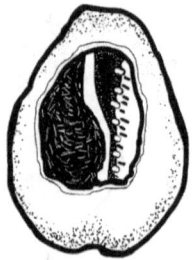  

OPEN SEGMENTS
/SPEAKING BELOW

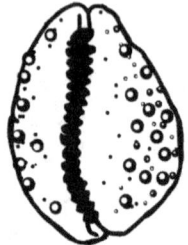 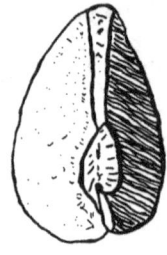 

Female   Male

Obi Abata creates the same patterns as Obi Agbon, which we described in Chapter eighteen: Alafia, Ejife, Etawa, Okanran, and Oyeku. However, Obi Abata distinguishes patterns based on male and female distinctions. Additionally, the Odu patterns in Obi Abata are named differently. In total, Obi Abata makes nine different patterns that we will discuss below.

Here is another image as shown below to also help you recognize the difference between both an open and closed kola nut segment.

Closed Segment   Open Segment

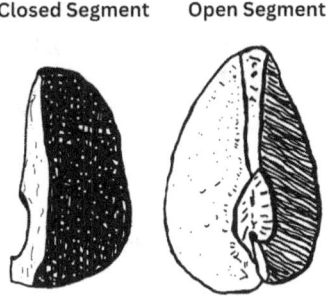

A four-lobed kola nut when separated into four pieces, consists of 2 male and 2 female pieces. Can you decipher the differences between the male and female pieces in the photo?

Open Male   Open Female
Segment   Segment

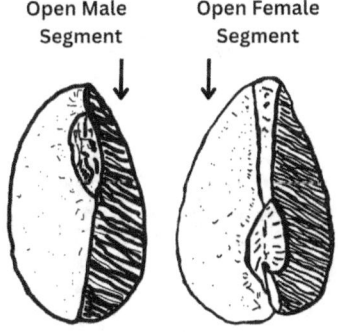

Below is another illustration showing how to distinguish between the male and female patterns in the Obi pieces. Note: Male and female combinations are interpreted only when the patterns are open; when they are closed, they are simply inter-preted as closed.

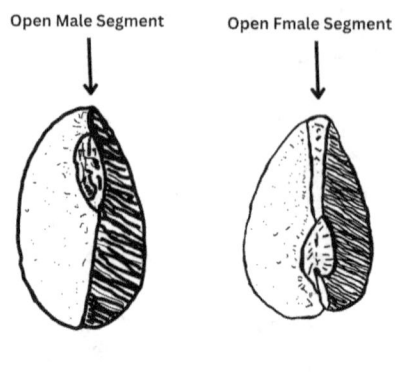

Open Male Segment   Open Fmale Segment

* * *

THE PATTERNS OF OBI ABATA

Now that you can hopefully distinguish between open, close male and female pieces of the Kola nut we will be looking at the various patterns that can be made when casting Obi Abata starting with Alafia-Ogbe.

THE PATTERN: ALAFIA-OGBE

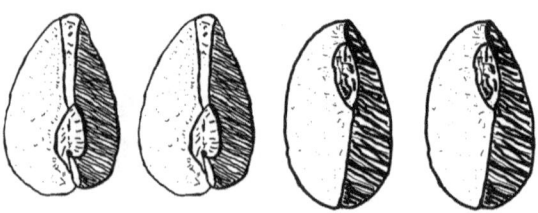

Alafia-Ogbe: All four segments of the kola nut are facing upwards. In this image, you can see two female segments on the left and two male segments on the right. The interpretation of Alafia-Ogbe is the same as Alafia, which often signifies blessings and positive energy flowing in a creative direction. Alafia is associated with Ire. The Orishas linked with Alafia-Ogbe are the same as those associated with Alafia. Please refer to the interpretation of Alafia in Chapter 18 for more details.

THE PATTERN: OYEKU

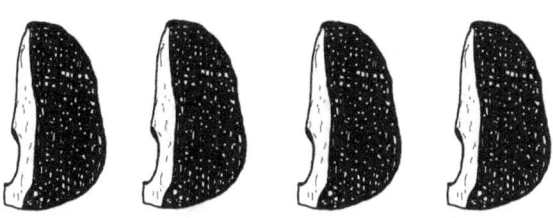

Oyeku: All four segments of the Kola Nut in this pattern are facing downwards and are in the closed position. Oyeku is often interpreted as confusion, the complete lack of light in a situation and needing to find a different direction. Refer to chapter 18 for further interpretation. Oyeku comes in Osogbo.

THE PATTERN: EJIFE-EJIRE

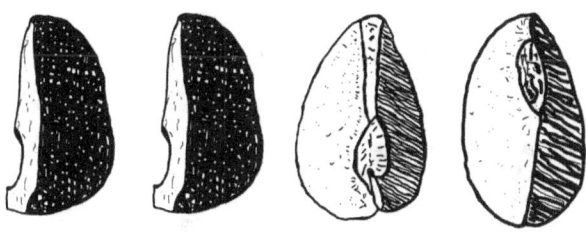

Ejife-Ejire: true ejife, is when you have 1 male open segment facing upwards and 1 open female segment also facing upwards and 2 segments in the downwards closed position. Ejife comes in Ire. The interpretation of Ejife-ejire is the same as Ejife. Ejife-ejire can often mean harmonious balance. Where both masculine and feminine energies exist, they often create harmony. Refer to the previous chapter for further interpretation under "Ejife

Ejife-Akoran: (male- ejife) is when you have 2 male open segments on the left facing upwards and 2 segments facing downwards in the closed position. Ejife comes in ire. Ejife-ako can often be interpreted as a balance and a good outcome but one in which will require competition, motivation, and strength to achieve. One may need to go out and get the opportunity rather than waiting for it to present itself.

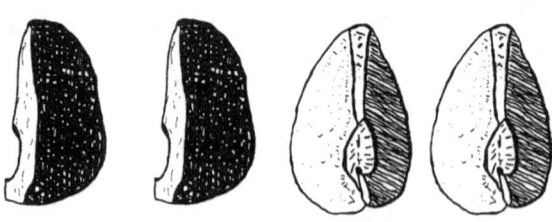

Ejife-Ero: (female - ejife) is when you have 2 female open segments facing upwards and 2 segments facing downwards in the closed position. This pattern comes in Ire. Ejife-ero can often be interpreted as a balance and a good outcome, but one in which will require more

nurturing, patience, guidance, and inner growth needing more feminine qualities to be able to achieve true balance and achieve a goal.
Ejife-ero often coms in ire.

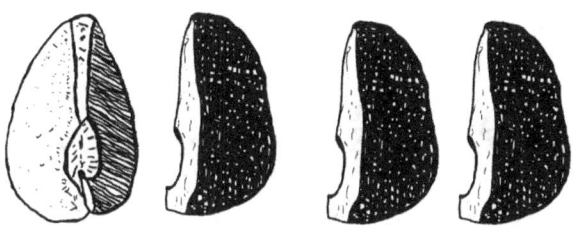

Okanran-Aje: is when you have 1 female open segment facing
upwards and 3 segments facing downwards in the closed position.
Okanran-aje is often seen as having the feminine qualities of nurturing, patience, guidance, and inner growth but lacking the masculine
qualities which include competition, motivation, and strength to
achieve a goal. Okanran comes in Osogbo.

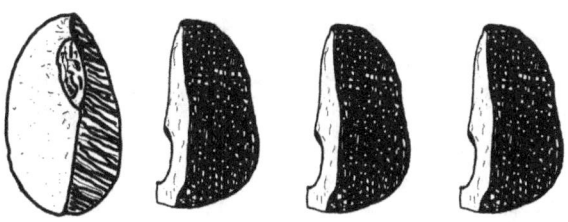

Okanran-Ilera: is when you have 1 male open piece facing upwards
and 3 other pieces in the closed downwards position. Okanran
comes in Osogbo. Okanran-Ilera is often seen as having the mascu-

line qualities of competition, motivation, and strength to achieve a goal but lacking the feminine qualities which include nurturing, patience, guidance, and inner growth. Okanran-ilera often comes in Osogbo.

THE PATTERN: ETAWA-AKITA

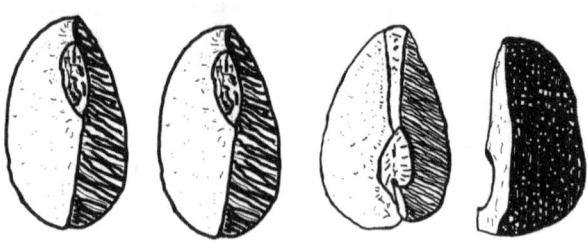

Etawa-Akita: is when you have 2 male open pieces facing upwards and 1 female segment facing upwards as well as 1 other piece in the closed downwards position. Etawa comes in Ire. Etawa-Akita still is seen as an imbalance however something is still lacking and unknown. This Odu ofen comes in ire.

THE PATTERN: ETAWA-OBITA

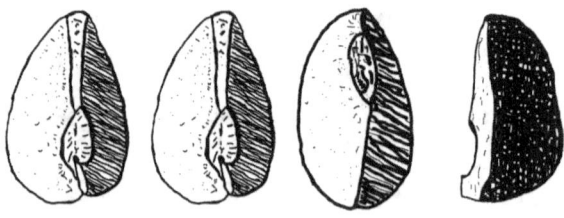

<u>**Etawa-obita:**</u> is when you have 2 female open pieces facing upwards and 1 male piece facing upwards as well as 1 other piece in the closed

downwards position. Etawa comes in Ire. Etawa-obita still is seen as an imbalance however, something is still lacking and unknown.

HOW TO CONSTRUCT AN
OBI ABATA REPLICA SET

In many parts of the world, traditional kola nuts are difficult to acquire, so some may consider alternatives. In the previous chapter, we explained how to create your own Obi set by sanding down several coconut pieces.

For this activity, you will follow steps 1 through 8 from the last chapter on how to construct an Obi set. However, you will add an extra step which will consist of painting or marking the pieces. with an X and an O. In the prior chapter, we discussed marking "X" and "O" to symbolize whether a segment is open or closed. In this activity, we will use "X" and "O" to represent male (X) and female (O). You will mark all four OPEN sides of each coconut piece with an X and an O making in total two Xs and two Os. This will provide you with all the combinations of the traditional Obi Abata.

Once you complete the prayers and the steps in the prior chapter, you can cast using this tool and read it just as you would with the traditional Obi Abata Kola nut.

* * *

CHAPTER 20

OSAIN AND THE USE OF PLANTS

THE YORUBA PEOPLE have a rich tradition of healing using plants, with healing being a significant component of Yoruba spirituality. Plants are utilized for various purposes, including protection, promoting health, and as offerings to the Orishas and ancestors. They are also crucial and necessary to every aspect of Yoruba spirituality and practice, from being used in rituals, initiations, and divination, to also being used for the creation of amulets, and the charging of sacred objects, to name just a few. The Yoruba believe that every plant possesses a particular type of Ase (power) that manifests within the plant as an energy matrix unique to the plant's natural purpose of existence and destiny. This energy matrix aligns with the Odu pattern the plant was born under as well. All plants on Earth are associated with a particular Odu, and often this pattern is visible in the appearance of the plant itself.

It is said that this Odu pattern that you can see in the form the plant takes is the energy matrix within it. The energy matrix of Ase also determines the form the plant takes and the healing or magical properties it possesses, not the other way around. Discovering the natural spiritual healing properties of plants often involves communication with the Orishas and divination. Each plant is frequently associated with a specific Orisha as well. In traditional Yoruba medicine, an incantation is recited over the herb or "ewe" to activate the plant's healing properties and to release its "Ase," which is believed to be dormant within the plant until activated. We do this by not only reciting an incantation but by crushing up the plant, breaking it into parts. In Yoruba, we call medicine by the term "ewe," which in English translates to the words "leaves or herbs". One of the most important deities in Yoruba spirituality, when it comes to the herbs or leaves, "ewe" is the Orisha Osain. He is viewed as a divine healer, botanist, and herbalist.

Osain is said to rule over all plant life and greenery. Orisha practitioners believe he knows the cures to all diseases and the secret uses of every plant. Osain is also rumored to have been created from the Ase that manifested through the union of water and soil during the creation of the world. Both Osain and Orunmila are often invoked by Priests when working with sacred herbs and medicines.

* * *

Important!

It is important to note that before handling unknown plants, identify them with a botanist, wear gloves, and wash your hands afterward. This book focuses solely on Yoruba spirituality and does not offer medical advice. Exercise caution before tasting or touching unfamiliar plants, ensuring proper identification to avoid harm. Discuss any herbal remedies with a medical provider to prevent allergic reactions or other complications.

* * *

In Yoruba traditional medicine, the term Olóògùn refers to a spiritual herbalist who holds a unique priestly authority, often recognized as being under the Orisha Osain. Sometimes Olóògùns are also Babalawos or Babalorishas if they have been initiated into the mysteries of Osain.

The journey toward healing often begins with a divination consultation led by a Babalorisha or Babalawo. This ritual takes precedence before considering herbal remedies. For the Yoruba, divination, coupled with the completion of Ebo (prescribed sacrifices), is viewed not just as a recommendation but as a transformative healing process, provided that the Ebos are diligently performed. A rich array of healing solutions may be suggested, ranging from Ebos and adimus to daily prayers and incantations. There's also the inclusion of Omiero, which is a blend of herbs and water suitable for body cleansing or adding to a bath. Additionally, a personalized soap called an *"Akose"* may be prescribed and made specifically for the client, crafted from a mix of herbs, oils, and natural elements tailored to meet the individual's specific needs based on what came up and what the client's needs are during the divination reading.

The Yoruba hold the belief that cleansing the body with specific herbs contributes to healing and removes negative energy from an individual's spiritual essence. Moreover, they believe in the nourishing and empowering effects of these natural remedies on a person's Ori, enhancing their spiritual vitality and bringing Ase, or life force, to the individual. According to Yoruba healing philosophy, physical illnesses are believed to arise from neglecting the spiritual self, often stemming from an imbalance or depletion of the life force and the individual's "Ase."

CLASSIFYING VARIOUS PLANTS AND HERBS

Classifying Various Plants and Herbs. Classifying plants and herbs by natural climate and elements can be useful when identifying them for their spiritual uses. Herbs can be classified by the type of energy they possess and the Odu associated with. I intend to show you a very useful tool for classifying plants. In the image below you have what are referred to as the five potencies: Warm, Damp, Dry, Neutral, and Cool.

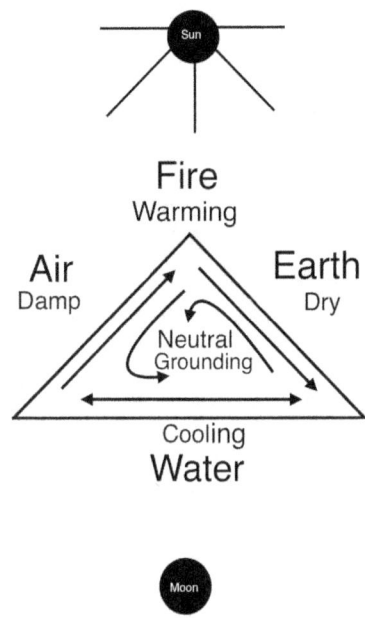

Warm plants are often categorized by the heat or spiciness they produce either in aroma or in taste. Dryness is often categorized by how woody a plant is and by the plant's lack of moisture. Dampness is often associated with plants or herbs that are more wet and have an increase in water content. Coolness is often associated with plants or herbs that are cool in their aroma or taste, like the mint family, or many fruits and vegetables that are refreshing, such as the cucumber family. Neutral herbs and plants are often equally mixed between Warm, Cool, Damp, and Dry and cannot be categorized specifically under these categories.

The five potencies classify plants by various natural climate variations that occur in nature. One would probably not ingest a dry, warm herb like cinnamon on a hot day, but instead seek a cool, damp herb like a lemon, an orange, or a cucumber to help eliminate heat from the body. The same can be said on a cold, damp winter day when perhaps hot ginger or cinnamon tea may be most refreshing. It is believed that balancing out moisture and heat, coolness in the body can help to rebalance the person's spiritual energies. It is often said that when someone has too much heat, they need more coolness.

Here are some examples of plants and herbs categorized under the five potencies:

- **Warm and Dry Plants:** Cinnamon, Clove, Black and Red Pepper, Mustard Seed,
- **Cool and Damp Plants**: Mint, Cucumber, Cilantro, Basil, Sage
- **Neutral and Damp Plants:** Parsley, Dill, Cool and Dry Plants: Rosemary, Thyme

Often, dry and warm herbs tend to be ruled more by sun energy, while damp and cool herbs tend to be ruled more by the energy of the moon and water.

MAKING SPIRITUAL BATHS

Creating a spiritual bath involves combining herbs, candles, plants, and other elements. Orisha practitioners use this ritual to promote healing, absorb energies from different Orishas for enhanced health and well-being, or to invite blessings. I often add various crystals to my spiritual baths; my favorite is to add some river rocks I got on a hike if I am making a bath in honor of the Orisha Oshun, or add some shells and sea salt to replicate the ocean in honor of Yemaya. I would suggest, however, that you first make sure before you add rocks or crystals to water to ensure they are clean and safe, as well as making sure the crystal or rock can be put in water without destroying it. Here are a few spiritual baths you can try:

* * *

Obatala's Tranquility Bath

Obatala: Bringer of peace, tranquility, calmness, rules over these energies. Herbs associated with Obatala are Cotton, Myrrh, Frankincense, Basil, white roses, Mint, Spearmint, Lavender, fennel.

Purpose: to honor Obatala and help bring peace, tranquility, calmness. This bath Includes the following:

A little creativity, (you can add your own creativity to this bath and let your Ori guide you. You can add or take away from the ingredients in this list. All these ingredients are optional)

- Quartz crystal or a piece of silver
- White Flower petals
- Some of the herbs mentioned above
- A dash of Coconut milk, regular milk, or rice water
- A dash of ground-up eggshell powder.
- Offering to Obatala: A white candle

Important: Avoid adding salts or alcohol to this bath due to the nature and taboos of Obatala. I recommend preparing an Omiero rather than just adding all these herbs and ingredients directly to your bath. You can prepare an Omiero by boiling a mix of herbs and ingredients in a kettle. Strain the boiled mixture and use the water for a bath. Following this, I also recommend you dedicate a small white candle to Obatala as an offering and then ask Obatala to bring tranquility, peace, and calmness into your life.

You may want to bottle up the Omiero and set it next to the small candle for a few days, each time lighting the candle and asking Obatala to bring tranquility, peace, healing, and calmness to you. You can use some of the Omiero herbal mixture for your bath while saving the rest for future baths as well if you choose.

Also, this process can be repeated for any of the Orishas and Spiritual baths on the following pages.

Yemaya's Nurturing Bath

Yemaya: bringer of nurturing energy, connection with the moon, self-love, emotional healing, and nurturing. Herbs associated with Yemaya are Seaweed, Kelp, lemon grass, ocean foam, shells, lettuce. Saltwater

A little creativity, (you can add your own creativity to this bath and let your Ori guide you. You can add or take away from the ingredients in this list. All these ingredients are optional)

Purpose: to honor Yemaya and help bring self-love, emotional healing, connection with the moon and the tides and self-nurturing as well as balance to your inner self/ inner waters. This bath Includes the following:

- Several Seashells
- 4 tablespoons of Sea salt or mineral salt
- Some of the herbs mentioned above
- A dash of ground-up eggshell powder.
- 2 tablespoons of brown sugar
- 1 teaspoon of lemon juice or a cut-up lemon
- Sea kelp or lettuce
- Offering to Yemaya: a small blue candle

* * *

<u>Oshun's Beauty Bath</u>

Oshun: bringer of beauty, love, sensuality, and fertility. Herbs associated with Oshun are Pumpkin, Chamomile, honey, Orange, melons, cinnamon, Dandelion, sunflowers, Bananas, Papaya.

A little creativity, (you can add your own creativity to this bath and let your Ori guide you. You can add or take away from the ingredients in this list. All these ingredients are optional)

Purpose: to honor Oshun and help bring beauty, love, sensuality, and fertility. This bath Includes the following:

- A River Stone (keep the river stone for future baths)
- 1 teaspoon of cinnamon or 2 cinnamon sticks
- Several tablespoons of Honey (optional) or Sugar to bring sweetness to your life.
- Orange/Grapefruit slices
- Yellow or Orange flower petals
- Red rose petals
- Eucalyptus or Sage leaves
- Dried raisins
- Offering to Oshun: a small yellow candle.

River water (This one is optional, make sure it is boiled and that it does not contain any microscopic parasites or dangerous contaminants. You can also use bottled spring water as well.

Note: do not add salt to this bath. Oshun is the mother of all the non-salt bodied of water.,

* * *

OGUN'S ENERGY BATH

Ogun: bringer of motivation, stamina, passion, perseverance, strength. Some herbs associated with Ogun are Snake plant, Eucalyptus, ginger, clove, black pepper, Iron, yams rum.

A little creativity, (you can add your own creativity to this bath and let your Ori guide you. You can add or take away from the ingredients in this list. All these ingredients are optional)

- Gin or Rum
- Fresh mint or sage
- A small pebble or rock found near the railroad tracks.
- Eucalyptus or ginger
- Offering to Ogun: a small green candle.

* * *

SHANGO'S PROTECTION BATH

Shango: bringer of masculine energy, balance, strength, self-esteem. Some herbs associated with Shango include Mango, Oak tree, Cayenne pepper, sage, okra, bananas.

A little creativity, (you can add your own creativity to this bath and let your Ori guide you. You can add or take away from the ingredients in this list. All these ingredients are optional)

- Some of the herbs mentioned above
- Rum or Gin
- 1 teaspoon of Coconut oil.
- 2 tablespoons of Sugar
- Offering to Shango afterwards to bring blessings of the bath: a small red or white candle.

* * *

Orunmila's Spiritual Bath

Orunmila: bringer of wisdom and insight, self-awareness and self-reflection and reflection on one's own life, ability to see the future and Psychic abilities. Some herbs associated with Orunmila include Coconut, palm leaves, Palm Kernels, red hibiscus, sage, Basil.

A little creativity, (you can add your own creativity to this bath and let your Ori guide you. You can add or take away from the ingredients in this list. All these ingredients are optional)

- Sage leaves
- Coconut water
- Basil leaves
- Mint leaves
- Rum or Gin
- A small amount of shea butter or palm oil.
- Offering afterwards to bring blessings: a small green or yellow candle.

* * *

Open roads Spiritual Bath

Elegua: bringer of youthful energy, playful energy, vitality and not to take things so seriously. Herbs associated with elegua include Tobacco, licorice, Rum, Plantain, Rosemary, Banana, Bermuda grass, lavender, guinea pepper, popcorn, guava, Anis, Lemon Balm, Coffee to name a few.

A little creativity, (you can add your own creativity to this bath and

227

let your Ori guide you. You can add or take away from the ingredients in this list. All these ingredients are optional)

- Rum or gin
- lavender, eucalyptus, or sage
- 1 teaspoon of Shea butter or coconut oil
- Honey or sugar
- Rosemary leaves
- 2 teaspoons of ground coffee beans
- Offering afterwards: a small black or red candle.

* * *

Elegua/ Eshu Offering Incense

This incense can be used to burn at the crossroads or near the entrance of your home as an offering to Elegua/Eshu. You can also offer Eshu a cup of black coffee and place it next to the door.

Ingredients include: One incense burner, one charcoal piece for burning incense, One Mortar and pestle for grinding the ingredients.

Incense includes: Tobacco (Optional and not required), Myrrh, Clove, Sandalwood (Optional), Black or red pepper, Honey.

* * *

Incense Recipe for Smudging and Clearing Negative Energy

Ingredients: 1 part Cinnamon, 1 part Sage, 1 part Mint, 1 fireproof bowl for burning.

Instructions: Combine equal parts of cinnamon, sage, and mint, Place the mixture in a fireproof bowl, Light the mixture and allow it to smolder, creating smoke, Use the smoke to smudge and clear negative energy from your space.

* * *

Oya's Spiritual Bath

Oya: bringer of determination to make the changes needed, ability to communicate with the dead and the ancestors, bringer of clairvoyant abilities and communication with the spirit world. Herbs associated with Oya include Eggplant, mugwort, snake plant, Papaya, lime, sandalwood, Nutmeg, clove, plums, raisins.

A little creativity, (you can add your own creativity to this bath and let your Ori guide you. You can add or take away from the ingredients in this list. All these ingredients are optional)

- Red wine
- Dried Raisins
- Lime or Lemon juice
- Amethyst Crystal (Helps to change the vibrational energy of the water)
- Red Rose Petals
- Offering to Oya afterwards: a small purple candle or some incense.

* * *

Oya's Offering Incense

Ingredients include: One incense burner, One charcoal piece for burning incense, One Mortar and pestle for grinding the ingredients.

Incense includes the following:

- 1 part frankincense,
- 1 part Myrrh,
- 1 Part Sandalwood (Optional),
- A few drops of honey (Optional),
- Add some dried Raisins.

I often used this simple incense recipe as an offering to both the ancestors as well as to the Orisha Oya.

* * *

ORI CLEARING SPIRITUAL BATH

Purpose: to cleanse and clear, strengthen, and feed one's Ori

Ingredients include:

- White flower petals
- Quartz crystal
- Coconut water
- Honey
- Shea butter
- A handful of dried Oats
- A little creativity, (you can add your own creativity to this bath and let your Ori guide you.
- No need to burn a candle for this bath. The bath is considered an offering to your Ori by itself.

* * *

A LIST OF COMMON ITEMS USED FOR
SPIRITUAL CLEANINGS

- **Florida Water**: A type of cologne to attract positive energy to your home or space. Added some water and a few drops of Florida water into a spray bottle to clean your home or space.
- **African Black Soap**: Believed to rid the body of negative impurities and help replenish the ori.
- **Efun:** White powder made from egg, often used to purify, or clean. Sometimes a small amount is added to a bath to help with purification. It can be sprinkled around the home to eliminate bad energy.
- **An Egg:** Eggs are sometimes used by Orisha practitioners to wash the body by rubbing egg over various parts of the body to cleanse and purify it. Following this, the egg is then discarded. If the egg happens to break it is likely due to strong energy. You can clean up the broken egg, throw it away and then get another egg and repeat the process.
- **Shea butter**: Often used in ceremonies and cleansings within the Orisha tradition. It is an offering often given to Ori, Obatala, and Orunmila.
- **Coconut milk**: An offering for various Orishas and to Ori.
- **Rainwater:** Believed to improve communication with Oya and the ancestors. Helps sharpen your psychic abilities as well as your inner guidance or intuition.

* * *

COMMON PLANTS ASSOCIATED WITH
DIFFERENT ORISHAS

- **Ogun:** Basil, Snake plant, Avocado, Siempre Viva (ewe dundun).

- **Ochosi**: Basil, Tobacco, Alacrancillo.
- **Babaluaye:** Salvia (Salvia salvia), Rosemary.
- **Shango:** Plantain leaves, Saw palmetto, Kapok tree (Ceiba pentandra), Okra, Ficus religiosa. Many of the herbs associated with Shango have pointed leaves that resemble an Edun Ara, commonly referred to as a thunder-stone.
- **Eshu**: Sugar cane, Guava, Licorice root, Dragon's blood, Copal, Anise, Rue.
- **Obatala**: White lily, Sage, Mint, Cotton, Rice, Clover.
- **Oya:** Mugwort, Geranium, Plum, Plum leaves, Camphor, Hibiscus, Sandalwood, Nutmeg, Clove, Codiaeum variegatum. Oya's sacred rattle may sometimes be made from the seed pods of Delonix regia. Plants with leaves that are multiple colors often belong to Oya.
- **Yemoja** : Lemongrass, Aloe vera, Lettuce, Seaweed, Zebrina pendula, Cucaracha.
- **Oshun:** Sunflowers, Roses, Marigolds, Cinnamon, Papaya, Myrrh.
- **Orunmila:** Coconut, Marigold, Clover, Sage.

COMMON RUE (RUTA GRAVEOLENS)
Uses: Rue is often used in herbal infusions to cleanse and purify objects, spaces, and people. Grind up fresh rue leaves, sage, and lavender leaves in cool water to make an Omiero. Use the branches of the rue plant, wet them with the water, and sprinkle the water in the four corners of a room to purify and cleanse it. You can also sprinkle the water on yourself or others to wash away bad spiritual energy.

* * *

MINT (MENTHA PIPERITA)
Uses: Grind up fresh mint leaves to make an omiero. You can wash

yourself with it to cool down your Ori. The fresh leaves of this herb are also good to leave on the top of your orishas to cool down heat. When doing divination, the omiero made of mint leaf and water can be sprinkled around the room or on the client's and diviner's head to cool down the intensity.

Siguaraya (Trichilia havanensis): This plant is commonly used for protection and is believed, especially in Cuba, to hold the powers of the seven major Orishas; Yemaya, Eleggua, Oshun, Obatala, Orunmila, Ogun, and Shango. Its leaves are often used for cleansing and seeking protection. The Orishas are thought to dwell within the branches of this tree, offering protection to its caretaker. Cutting down this tree is often forbidden. If you encounter one, it is customary to leave a small offering beneath it and ask for a blessing from one of the seven Orishas.

In conclusion, the Yoruba have a rich and ancient tradition of herbal healing and traditional medicine that is an important aspect of their spirituality. Their rich heritage continues to help us and guide us today.

* * *

CHAPTER 21

FINDING A SPIRITUAL COMMUNITY

CONGRATULATIONS ON REACHING the final chapter of your journey! Now that you have completed all the chapters in this book, you should have a solid foundation in Yoruba tradition and spirituality. I hope you enjoyed this book as much as I enjoyed writing it. I wish you well on your spiritual journey, and I hope this book serves as a valuable resource for you and for those you share it with.

Finding a supportive community may require patience. Not everyone has genuine intentions, so it's crucial to exercise caution in your search. As the saying goes, "not all that glitters is gold," especially true in online settings where authenticity can be challenging to discern. When seeking mentors and groups online, always prioritize your intuition and follow these guidelines for a successful journey:

1. **Firstly, trust yourself and your instincts**: If something feels off, it's okay to walk away, even while showing respect to elders.
2. **Seek a community that shares your values and offers sincere support**: This search may take time, but it is vital for your spiritual growth.

3. **Orisha spirituality should never instill fear:** Steer clear of anyone who uses fear tactics, particularly those who demand payment to dispel curses. Legitimate practitioners are transparent about costs and uphold ethical standards.

4. **Learning is an ongoing process in this tradition:** Continuously expand your knowledge through study to deepen your spiritual growth and make well-informed decisions about your path.

5. **Respect the rituals, ceremonies, and practices passed down through generations, guarding against cultural appropriation and exploitation whenever possible:** It is important to engage with local communities and practitioners face-to-face for trustworthy and meaningful interactions; this is the most effective way one can spiritually develop. Orisha spirituality is not a solitary practice.

6. **Remember, consistent practice, even in small amounts**, is more beneficial than infrequent, lengthy sessions, as it helps maintain a continuous spiritual connection.

Congratulations once more on reaching this milestone! Throughout your journey, you have cultivated a profound respect for the rituals and ceremonies central to Ifa and Orisha practices. As you move forward, embrace the excitement of discovery and the fulfillment of spiritual awakening. Your journey is unique and personal; may it lead you to profound insights, boundless joy, and a deeper connection to the divine.

* * *

May Olodumare continue to bless you, give you support, and guide you on your journey.

The End

* * *

GLOSSARY

A

- **Abiku**: A spirit that is repeatedly born into the human world but does not wish to live a full human life, typically dying in childhood. (Chapter 4).
- **Adimú**: A food offering made to the Orishas or ancestors. (Chapter 16).
- **Aganju**: The Orisha of the wilderness and difficult terrains. Also, a historical king of the Oyo empire. (Chapter 3).
- **Agbon**: Coconut. (Chapter 18).
- **Aje**: The Orisha and spirit of money, wealth, and prosperity. (chapter 3)
- **Ajogun:** Demonic and destructive entities that bring chaos and disharmony. They feed off energy that lingers around a person who has done negative deeds and has bad character.
- **Akose**: A combination of materials, often herbs and other natural items, containing Ase used for healing, medicine, or cleansing. (Chapter 20).

- **Akunlegba**: The part of a person's ori that holds the innate qualities given in heaven, such as intelligence.
- **Akunleyan**: The part of the ori that controls conscious desires, dreams, wishes, and hopes.
- **Alafia**: Good luck in Obi divination (when four pieces land face up). (Chapter 18, 19).
- **Aleyo**: A newcomer to the Orisha religion.
- **Ara**: The human world (Earth).
- **Araba**: An Ifa Priest who is also a Chief.
- **Aro/Arun**: Disease or illness.
- **Ase**: Spiritual power to manifest change.
- **Atari**: The crown of the head, connecting your Ori to the divine.
- **Atunwa**: The concept of being reborn ("to return," "repetition"). (Chapter 4).
- **Awó**: Secret knowledge held by initiates, a title referring to someone who is initiated in Ifa.
- **Ayangalu**: (Variant?) A lesser-known Orisha associated with crossroads. (chapter 3)
- **Ayanmo**: Unchangeable destiny (fixed qualities).
- **Ayé**: The physical world, contrasted with the spiritual

B

- **Baba**: "Father" (a respectful term used in family and religious contexts).
- **Babaloricha/Babalocha**: A respected Santero with extensive initiation knowledge.
- **Babalawo**: A skilled diviner and spiritual guide, also known as a priest of Orula.
- **Babalú Ayé**: The Orisha of diseases, epidemics, and leprosy. (Chapter 3)
- **Batá**: A set of three double headed drums resembling an

hourglass, each with specific roles and spiritual significance.

- **Bembé**: A lively drumming ceremony held in honor of the Orishas.
- **Boveda**: An altar dedicated to ancestors and spirits, used for offerings and prayers.
- **Burukú**: Moral flaws or bad character ("iwá burukú").

C

- **Candomblé**: Afro-Brazilian religion with Yoruba influences and rituals. (Chapter 1).
- **Cowrie**: A type of seashell used in divination and ceremonies, symbolizing wealth, money and used as currency by the ancient Yoruba. (Chapter 18, 19).

D

- **Dada**: An Orisha associated with motherhood, fertility, and well-being of unborn children. (Chapter 3).
- **Derecho**: Payment made to Olorisha or Babalawo for their services or out or respect.

E

- **Ebo**: Sacrifice or offering made to an Orisha or Spirit. (Chapter 16).
- **Eboriru**: Often practiced by Orisha priests, especially Babalawos, it involves prayers (Adura) and may include both Ebo Eje (blood sacrifice) and Adimu (food offerings). This method is viewed as the traditional way of offering Ebo by some Orisha practitioners.
- **Egbe**: Refers to a group, society, or community in heaven.

- **Egún**: Spirits of deceased ancestors (some lineages include religious significance).
- **Egungun**: Masquerade costumes worn to honor the Egun (ancestor) spirits.
- **Eewo**: A person's spiritual taboos or forbidden actions, connected to the Ori (spirit) called Eewo.
- **Efun**: A white powder often made from crushed seashells or eggs, used for religious purposes like purification, offerings, and body markings.
- **Elegua / Eshu**: An Orisha associated with crossroads and roads. (Chapter 3).
- **Emi**: The soul, spirit, or essence of a person.
- **Emi**: The human soul, believed to be composed of several parts (more specifics may be needed).
- **Erinle**: An Orisha associated with healing, hunting, and water, also known as Inle. (Chapter 3).
- **Ese**: Verses of Odu which are often sung or chanted by Ifa Priests during divination or sacrifice.
- **Esentaye**: Ceremony meaning "Feet touch the ground," performed for newborns within the first 16 weeks.
- **Etutu**: Offering to ancestors, often in the form of Adimu (ritual food offering).
- **Ewe**: Leaves or herbs used in medicinal practices, known as "ewe" in Yoruba. (Chapter 20).

F

- **Funeral Rites / Itutu**: Ceremonies honoring and guiding the deceased within the Yoruba tradition.
- **Funfun**: Meaning white, often associated with the Orisha Obatala.
- **Fúnke**: Spiritual blessing or essence given by Orishas or ancestors

- **Ibeji**: Orisha represented as divine twins, typically gifted to devotees as two statues, one male and one female. (Chapter 3).
- **Ibori**: A ceremony performed on someone to help strengthen and elevate their Ori/consciousness.
- **Ifa**: A divination system originating among the Yoruba consisting of 256 Odu or signs. Ifa plays a large role in the broader Yoruba spiritual tradition. (Chapter 15).
- **Igbeyawo**: Yoruba traditional wedding ceremony.
- **Igbodú**: Sacred space often used during initiations.
- **Igbó (Ibo)**: Small sacred tools such as shells and bones used by a priest to help them determine the orientation of the Odu during divination.
- **Igba Iwa**: A calabash believed to contain all the energies in creation.
- **Igi**: A stick.
- **Igoke**: Spiritual development or evolution that takes place when one is in alignment with their destiny.
- **Ikin:**Sacred palm nuts, seeds with four eyes or more used in Ifa divination.
- **Ileke**: Beads worn by Orisha devotees.
- **Ilé**: House, often refers to a house or community of Orisha practitioners.
- **Ipadawaye**: which means "the ancestor has returned," is often used when a child is reborn. There is a belief that when a child comes into the world, they are a reborn ancestor.
- **Ipako**: Reservoir of spiritual power (ase) within your Ori. (Chapter 8).
- **Iponri**: Part of the soul connected to heaven, the higher self, spiritual twin in heaven. (Chapter 8).

- **Ipese**: Means to appease and make things right, sometimes used to refer to an offering given to the Iyami.
- **Iroke:** called the Ifa divination tapper resembles a tusk of an animal with carved images in it. Traditionally they were made of ivory but today they are often made of wood or deer antlers.
- **Iroko**: Spirit dwelling in the Iroko tree (Milicia Excelsa) in Africa.
- **Irukere**: A horsetail whisk used by priests for cleansing the space prior to performing rituals or divination.
- **Irunmole**: Primordial beings created by Olodumare before the world existed.
- **Ire**: Blessings, being in alignment with a person's destiny, good fortune, and positive energy.
- **Ire Aiku**: Long life, good health (major blessing).
- **Itadogun**: 16-day divination period in the Yoruba calendar.
- **Itutu**: Offering to elevate and cool the deceased spirit, also used to refer to funeral rites honoring and guiding the recently deceased person.
- **Itéfa**: Full Ifa initiation.
- **Iwa**: Human character (iwa rere = good character). (Chapter 13).
- **Iwa-inu**: Represents our inner character, embodying moral consciousness and spiritual strength.
- **Iwa pele**: Good character or behavior. (Chapter 13).
- **Iya**: "Mother".
- **Iyaami**: "My mothers," often refers to a group of female Orishas and spirits.
- **Iyalorisha**: Female Orisha priestess.
- **Iyanifa**: Female Ifa priestess.
- **Iyabó (Iyawó)**: Novice initiate in Regla de Ocha (restrictions).
- **Iyalorisha (Iyalocha)**: Female Olorisha who initiates others.

- **Iyerosun**: Sacred powder used in divination and rituals.

K

- **Kehinde:** A name often given to "the second-born of twins."
- **Kola:** A bitter nut often used in Obi divination and as an offering.
- **Kójǫ́dá:** The traditional Yoruba calendar, meaning "may the day be clearly foreseen."

L

- **lódè:** refers to "outside" .
- **Lucumi / Lukumi:** An Afro-Cuban syncretic religious tradition that developed among descendants of Yoruba people.

M

- **Madrina:** Often refers to a godmother in the Lucumí/ Santeria tradition.
- **Meiji:** Refers to the number "two".
- **Merindinlogun:** Refers to the number "sixteen", the system of cowrie shell divination used by Orisha priests and priestesses.
- **Mojuba:** A prayer to ancestors and the Orishas asking for their support.

N

- **Nana Buluku:** She is commonly worshiped in Benin and Dahomey by the Fon people. She is considered the supreme goddess who gave birth to Mawu and Lisa in many Vodou lineages. (Chapter 3).

O

- **Oba**: Refers to a king or traditional ruler. It is also used as a title of respect for an Oriate, a master of ceremonies in certain rituals. (Chapter 3).
- **Obatala**: The Orisha of peace and purity. (Chapter 3).
- **Obanla:** Another name for the Orisha Obatala, meaning "praise the white cloth. (Chapter 3).
- **Obi**: A divination system using kola nut or coconut. Obi is also regarded as an Orisha. (Chapter 18, 19).
- **Oche / Oshe:** A double-headed ax that holds symbolic significance in association with the Orisha Sango.
- **Ode**: Means "outside" or "outer." (Chapter 8).
- **Odu**: Represents the womb, a divination pattern, or a pattern created by energy. It also refers to the verses or signs used in divination. (Chapter 14, 15, 18 19)
- **Oduduwa**: Viewed as both a historical Yoruba king and an Orisha who played a role in the creation myth, ruling over Ife, the city-state from which the Yoruba empire originated. (Chapter 3)
- **Ofo**: Refers to a sudden loss.
- **Ogbanje**: A spirit of a child believed to be born and die repeatedly.
- **Ogun**: The Orisha of iron, war, and technology. (Chapter 3).
- **Oke**: Often associated with the Orisha Obatala, with whom he is said to be inseparable. Oke is linked to extremely high mountains, peaks, and natural places. (Chapter 3).
- **Oko**: Associated with agriculture and farming, called upon by farmers and agriculturalists. Oko is also connected with the land and is considered the patron Orisha of farmers. (Chapter 3).
- **Olodumare**: The supreme creator deity, another name for God. (Chapter 2).
- **Olofin:** The ruler of heaven in Ifa tradition. (Chapter 2).

- **Olokun:** Orisha of the ocean and depths. (Chapter 2, 3).
- **Olorisha:** Initiated priest or priestess of Santería/Lucumi.
- **Olorun:** Sky god or another name for Olodumare. (Chapter 2).
- **Omi tutu:** A prayer offering fresh water to the Divinities; "fresh water."
- **Omi:** Water, offered as libation to the Orishas. (Chapter 20).
- **Omiero:** Sacred water mixed with herbs and natural ingredients for ceremonies, healing, and initiations. (Chapter 20).
- **Omo:** Means "child."
- **Omoluabi:** A person known for their good character and principles.
- **Opele:** A divination chain used in Ifa for spiritual guidance. (Chapter 15).
- **Opon Ifa:** A divination tray used in Ifa. (Chapter 15).
- **Oriate:** A priest revered for their mastery of ceremonies, especially in leading initiations, also known as an Oba (chief).
- **Orún:** Heaven or the spiritual realm, contrasting with Ayé, the earthly realm. (Chapter 2).
- **Ori-apere:** The unchanging aspect of a person's destiny. (Chapter 8).
- **Ori Inu:** The inner consciousness or inner head. (Chapter 8).
- **Ori:** The head or spiritual consciousness of an individual. (Chapter 8).
- **Oriki:** Praise, prayers, and songs used to honor ancestors, Orishas, or request blessings.
- **Orisha:** Deities in the Yoruba religious tradition.
- **Oro:** Oro was a historical king and is also seen as an Orisha of justice.
- **Orunmila:** Orisha of divination and wisdom. (Chapter 3).
- **Osain:** Orisha of the forest, herbs, and healing. (Chapter 3).

- **Osha / Ocha:** Shortened form of Orisha.
- **Oshosi:** Orisha of the forest, justice, and hunting. (Chapter 3).
- **Oshun:** Orisha of love, beauty, and rivers. (Chapter 3).
- **Osogbo:** Often refers to "negative energy" and being off track with one's destiny.
- **Osumare:** An Orisha of the Rainbow and the serpent. (Chapter 3).
- **Osun:** An Orisha that protects a person's Ori. (Chapter 3).
- **Otá (Otán):** Refers to certain stones representing spiritual energies.
- **Oti:** Alcohol often used in ceremonies, referring to hard spirits like gin.
- **Owo:** Represents money, wealth, or material blessings.
- **Oya:** Orisha of wind, storms, and the marketplace. (Chapter 3).
- **Oyin:** Means "honey."
- **Oyo:** A city in Nigeria.(Chapter 1,2).
- **Oyugbona:** Often used to refer to a person's "second godparents" in the religion.

P

- **Padrino:** Godfather.
- **Pagugu:** Also called the Ancestors staff or an Egun walking Stick, commonly used to help call upon the ancestors by tapping on the ground nine times.
- **Palo Mayombe:** an Afro-Cuban religion from Congo, venerates Nkisi spirits representing nature and life aspects through rituals and herbal medicine. (Chapter 1).
- **Pataki:** A sacred story or Yoruba myth often passed down and taught by word of mouth.

R

- **Regla de Ocha**: Also known as Santería or Lucumí, this religion originates from Yoruba people and was brought to Cuba and other parts of the America.

S

- **Sango**: Orisha associated with thunder and lightning in Yoruba religion, symbolizing power and strength. (Chapter 3).
- **Santería:** also known as Santería or Lucumí, is an Afro-Cuban religion rooted in Yoruba traditions. It originated in Cuba and spread to other parts of the Americas, blending elements of Catholicism, Taino (Indigenous Caribbean) beliefs, and other spiritual traditions alongside its Yoruba foundation. (Chapter 1).
- **Sopera**: A container used to house the Orisha and their sacred objects.

T

- **Tabi:** meaning "or" in this or that. Often used when asking a question in divination.
- **Taiwo:** A name often given to the first-born of twins.
- **Trinidad Orisha:** A syncretic Yoruba-based tradition that originated in Trinidad and Tobago. (Chapter 1).
- **Tutu**: Coolness.

U

- **Umbanda:** Originating in Brazil, Umbanda combines elements of African, indigenous, and Christian beliefs. It centers on the worship of the orishás. (Chapter 1).

V

- **Vodou:** Also known as Voodoo, Vodou is a syncretic religion that originated in Haiti. It centers on the worship of loas, spirits who represent various aspects of nature and human life and incorporates elements of West African religions. (Chapter 1).

W

- **Warriors:** An initiation ceremony where the Orishas Elegua, Ogun, Ochosi, and Osun are bestowed upon individuals to assist them on their spiritual journey.

Y

- **Yeye:** Another word for mother.
- **Yoruba:** An ethnic tribal people located in Nigeria known for their rich cultural heritage, language and religious traditions. (Chapter 1).

* * *

INDEX

Introduction

Who are the Yoruba?

Chapter 1

The Creation Story

Yoruba History: From Ile Ife to the Oyo Empire

The Slave Trade

Religious and Cultural Syncretism

A List of African Syncretic Religions, From Conflict to Modernization.

Chapter 2

The Yoruba Concept of God

Olodumare

Olorun

Olofin

Our Relationship with the Orishas

Who are the Irunmole?

What is the Sacred Duality?

Chapter 3

How the Orishas Acquired Their Powers, Descriptions of the Most Common Orishas: Aganju, Aje, Ayangalu, Babalu-Aye, Dada, Erinle, Esu/Elegua, Ibeji, Iroko, Nana Buluku, Oba, Obatala, Oduduwa, Ogun, Oke, Oko, Olokun, Olori-Merin, Orunmila, Osain, Oshosi, Oshun, Osumare, Oya, Shango, Yemaya, Yewa.

Chapter 4

Atunwa

Who are the Abiku?

Chapter 5

The Egungun Masquerade

The Orisha Oro

The Distinction Between Egun and Iwin

Guardian Ancestors

Other Orishas and Their Relationship to Egun

Chapter 6

The Egun Tile (Teja de Egun)

Building a Place to Honor Your Ancestors

What is Sacred Space?

Opening the Shrine

Closing the Shrine

Why Do We Call Forth Our Ancestors to Support Us?

What Should I Give to My Ancestors?

Regional and National Egun

Various Types of Prayers

Chapter 7

What is Umbanda?

What is a Boveda?

Constructing an Ancestors' Shrine

Reading Bubbles in Water

Divination Using Playing Cards

Chapter 8

How is Consciousness Defined in Yoruba Spirituality?

The Parts of Ori-inu

Ayanmo, Akunlegba, Akunleyan, Eewo

What is the Iponri?

On the Topic of Emi

Determining Alignment and Destiny

The Journey from Heaven to Earth

The Ori Alignment Ceremony

Other Food Items Offered to Ori

Chapter 9

The Traditional Yoruba Calendar

The Seven-Day Week Cycle for Observance

The Moon Phases and Their Meanings

Yoruba Festivals and Celebrations

Chapter 10

Dreams

The Role of Our Iponri or Spiritual Twin

Who are the Egbe-Orun?

Egbe Communities

Chapter 11

The Yoruba Life Cycle

The Naming Ceremony

Marriage

At Death

Chapter 12

Yoruba Initiation Rites and the Priestly Roles

What is Orisha Initiation?

Why Do People Get Initiated?

Working with the Orishas

Responsibilities of Initiates

Ori Ceremony

Honoring Egbe-Orun

Receiving Orishas

Itéfa/Ifa

The Role and Responsibilities of a Priest

Chapter 13

Understanding Iwa-pele and Omoluabi

Chapter 14

The Purpose of Divination

The Role of a Diviner

A Diviner's Responsibilities Towards Clients

Chapter 15

Decoding Odu Ifa

Understanding Ese Ifa

The Tools of Ifa

The Sixteen Major Odus of Ifa and Their Descriptions

Chapter 16

Sacrifice and Ebo

Types of Sacrifices

Emergency Offerings List

Chapter 17

Ire and Ibi

A List of Different Types of Ire and Ibi

Chapter 18

The Story of the Orisha Obi

The History of Obi Divination

How to Divine with Cowrie Shells

How to Ask Questions

When Needing to Ask More Than One Question

How to Make Your Own Obi Set

The Prayers for Invoking Obi

Chapter 19

Understanding Obi Abata

How to Use and Interpret Obi Abata

Chapter 20

Osain and the Use of Plants

Classifying Various Plants and Herbs

Making Spiritual Baths

A List of Common Items Used for Spiritual Cleanings

Common Plants Associated with Orishas

Chapter 21

Finding a Spiritual Community

Guidelines for a Successful Journey

BIBLIOGRAPHY

1. Abimbola, Wande. *Ifa Divination Poetry*. Translated, edited, and with an introduction by Wande Abimbola. NOK Publishers, 1977.
2. Adesola, Oluseye, and Philip Adedotun Ogundeji. "Chapter 17. Time in Yorùbá Perspective." *Data-Rich Linguistics: Papers in Honor of Yiwola Awoyale*, Cambridge Scholars Publishing, 2018.
3. Babayemi, S. O. *Egungun among the Oyo Yoruba*. University of Ibadan, 1980.
4. Bascom, William. *Ifa Divination: Communication Between Gods and Men in West Africa*. Indiana University Press, 1969.
5. Bascom, William R. *The Yoruba of Southwestern Nigeria*. Holt, Rinehart and Winston Waveland Press, 1969.
6. Blanco Torrealba, Isaac Omar. *Primeros Pasos de Un Omo Awo*. 2nd ed., 2016.
7. Cortez, J. G. *The Osha: Secrets of the Yoruba-Lucumi-Santeria Religion in the United States and the Americas*. Athelia Henrietta Press, 2000.

8. Dayrell, E., and A. Lang. *Folk Stories from Southern Nigeria*. Longmans, Green, and Co., 1910.

9. Ellis, A. B. *Yoruba-Speaking Peoples of the Slave Coast of West Africa: Their Religion, Manners, Customs, Laws, Language, etc.* Chapman and Hall, 1894.

10. Epega, A. *Obi: The Mystical Oracle of Ifa Divination*. Imole Oluwa Institute, 1985.

11. Falconbridge, A. *An Account of the Slave Trade on the Coast of Africa*. Printed by J. Phillips, 1788.

12. Gaitsn, T. *Vocabulario Santero*. Ediciones Orishas de Cuba, 1994.

13. Garcia Cortez, J. *The Osha II*. Athelia Henrietta Press, 2006.

14. Ibie, C. O. *Ifism: Complete Works of Orunmila*. Vol. 2, Athelia Henrietta Press, 1992.

15. Mullen, N. *Yoruba Art and Culture*. Exhibition catalog, Phoebe A. Hearst Museum of Anthropology, University of California, Berkeley, 2004.

16. Ogundiran, A. *The Yoruba: A New Perspective*. Indiana University Press, 2020.

17. Olaoluwa, S. "Postcolonial Contention and Cosmopolitan Temporality in Niyi Osundare's *Days*." *disClosure: A Journal of Social Theory*, vol. 25, 2016.

18. Oluwole-Olusegun, P. *History of the Yoruba People: Culture and Tradition*, Published online on Academia, 2020.

19. Osundiya, B. *Awo Obi: Obi Divination in Theory and Practice*. Athelia Henrietta Press, 2001.

20. Oyeweso, S., and O. C. Adesina, editors. *Ọ̀yọ́: History, Tradition, and Royalty: Essays in Honour of His Imperial Majesty the Alaafin of Ọ̀yọ́, Oba (Dr.) Lamidi Olayiwola Adeyemi III*. Ibadan University Press, 2021.

21. Smith, R. S. *Kingdoms of the Yoruba*. University of Wisconsin Press, 1969.

22. Sogbesan, O. "Primordial Yoruba Concept of Time and

Calendar: The Case of the Aboòrìsàs of Oyo Town." *Journal of Culture, Society and Development*, vol. 67, 2022.

ABOUT THE AUTHOR

Michael Perez, known as Awo Ayodele Ifagbemi, is a priest of the Yoruba spiritual tradition and a devoted practitioner of Orisha spirituality and Ifa divination. With a background in social work and over two decades of experience in spiritual exploration, he is committed to guiding others on their journey of healing, self-discovery, and personal transformation. Through his teachings, he shares the wisdom of the Orishas, offering a path to spiritual alignment and deeper understanding. In addition to *The Yoruba Spiritual Training Manual*, he is the author of *The Sacred Verses of the Orishas* and other works on Yoruba spirituality.